Real Estate Transactions and Foreclosure Control —A Home Mortgage Reference Handbook

THE CAUSES AND REMEDIES OF FORECLOSURE PAINS

FRANK M. IGAH, PH.D.

REAL ESTATE TRANSACTIONS AND FORECLOSURE CONTROL—A HOME MORTGAGE REFERENCE HANDBOOK

iUniverse books may be ordered through booksellers or by contacting:

iUniverse
1663 Liberty Drive
Bloomington, IN 47403
www.iuniverse.com
1-800-Authors (1-800-288-4677)

Because of the dynamic nature of the Internet, any web addresses or links contained in this book may have changed since publication and may no longer be valid. The views expressed in this work are solely those of the author and do not necessarily reflect the views of the publisher, and the publisher hereby disclaims any responsibility for them.

Any people depicted in stock imagery provided by Thinkstock are models, and such images are being used for illustrative purposes only.
Certain stock imagery © Thinkstock.

ISBN: 978-1-4917-2624-2 (sc)
ISBN: 978-1-4917-2666-2 (hc)
ISBN: 978-1-4917-6455-8 (e)

Library of Congress Control Number: 2014903360

Print information available on the last page.

iUniverse rev. date: 06/04/2015

Dedication

THIS BOOK IS DEDICATED TO MY
LOVELY WIFE AND CHILDREN.

TO THE MEMORY OF MY LATE PARENTS,

WHO VALUED EDUCATION TO
THE UTMOST LEVEL,

MAY THEIR SOULS REST IN PEACE.

ALSO, I DEDICATE THIS BOOK TO
MY BROTHERS AND SISTERS

Acknowledgement

Thanks to the individuals who helped with my book in many ways. They offered services, assistance and cooperation to the book. The first person is my spouse, *(Flora O. Igah, PhD, CRC)*. Her constructive criticisms and suggestions helped steer me to many significant and thoughtful ideas. Special thanks to my children, Frances "Chi-chi" C. Igah, (BS, MS) and Flora "Princess" E. Igah, (BS, MS, Doctoral candidate). They handled most of the computer works in the book. Moreover, sincere recommendations and deep assistance are offered to me by my other children named Dr. Katherine Ada Igah, Roswitha O. Igah, Doctoral candidate Madonna O. Igah and Frank, M. Igah Jr. I appreciate the encouragement and spiritual support received from my brother, Engr. Edward U. Igah and his wife Felicia Igah, my sisters Philomena O. Igah and Bridget N. with Joe Emelife, my parents-in-law Raymond and Maria Offiah, brothers and sisters in-laws, nephews, nieces, cousins and finally, my family friends including Peter and Roswitha Dilger (Western Germans).

I extend warm appreciation to the Realtors and Financial Professionals who responded to my investigative interrogations. I finally send gratitude to home owners, buyers and sellers that will read this book.

Front Matters
Overview Of The Chapters

FRONT MATTERS

1. The following information introduces the front matters. This book has twelve chapters. The twelfth chapter contains a summary with recommendations.

CHAPTER TWO

2. Chapter two introduces the real estate industry, audience, main objective and the author. The author outlines his knowledge, skills, experiences, abilities and unique qualification. This chapter explains the importance of home purchases. After reading this text, the readers will understand the readers Mortgage Loans, Real Estate Purchase Contracts and the Significance of this work.

CHAPTER THREE

3. Home mortgage and real estate transactions are well defined in this chapter. Home purchase ownership financing is described. Chapter three explains the etiology of real estate in the United States of America. In the beginning (1976), the land, garden and trees have been issued to the citizens by the Federal government. Also, the Federal government purchased many land from 1780 – 1865. The text of land ordinances are in chapter three.

CHAPTER FOUR

4. Chapter four explains the core activities for "Before" mortgage financing. This chapter, also, explains ratio analysis, case examples, business risk and financial risk in mortgage transactions. Finally, personal financing success can be summarized by Character, Capacity, Collateral, Condition, Communication and Industry Deceits.

CHAPTER FIVE

5. Chapter five explains "Frauds," "Cheating," and property theft against home buyers. The types of frauds are "higher profit" and "property theft." Some frauds and activities come in the form of flipping, lies, lumping, misleading and predatory lending. Finally, the home buyers and owners are explained to them as Legal Rights or Acts (Laws) for home actions. This action will help to educate real estate buyers, sellers and home owners.

CHAPTER SIX

6. Chapter six shows necessary actions for "During" mortgage financing. In most cases in the real estate industry, a purchase financing of less than fifty thousand dollars is not lucrative and not accepted. Moreover, mortgage financing have first, second and third levels of funding sources. Also, mortgage products or resources include Veteran Administration Conventional Mortgage, Package Mortgage, Blanket Mortgage, Budget Mortgage, land contract Mortgage and balloon contract Mortgage.

CHAPTER SEVEN

7. Chapter seven educates the home owners on actions to engage in "After" mortgage financing. Also, this chapter emphasizes the importance of keeping up with the monthly payments. Lenders understand as primary sources of risk for home owners. Further, security risks and diagram illustrations are Common stocks, Preferred stocks, Loans, and Real Estate stocks. Also, investment issuing channels which have been collaborated the classification of security loans are listed as well.

CHAPTER EIGHT

8. The most significant issues of Foreclosures with Repossessions are described in chapter eight. This chapter affects foreclosure causes, repossession pains, interest rates, remedy control and insurance protection. In this chapter, the author writes about how to stop or mitigate foreclosure damages and/or pains. This chapter concludes by mandating all citizens, especially home buyers and owners, to take the suggested actions to eliminate unfair practices, unjust actions and foreclosure punishments. In most cases, a home owner with foreclosure and repossession may suffer homelessness, acute poverty, Hopeless hunger and more. Finally, this book portrays how best to take care of owner sufferings from foreclosure and repossession.

CHAPTER NINE

9. The ninth chapter introduces and explains a new concept called the Real Estate Foreclosure Accommodation (REFA) program. The program's objective is to reshuffle mortgage financing and accommodate foreclosures with repossession. A mortgage in default is reshuffled during refinancing and with special features, rates and calculations which are uniquely related to the foreclosure victims. Moreover, if the REFA program is successfully accomplished, the result will give birth to "Reshuffled Mortgage Financing" (RMF). RMF mortgage is a newly structured deal that will permit a foreclosure victim to move back into his or her home with less demanding an affordable agreement.

CHAPTER TEN

10. Reverse Mortgage Program (RMP) is explained in details. The program is structured to reverse the payment of a mortgage. This program is introduced to assist home owners with an alternative way to avoid foreclosure with repossession. The home owner instead of making a mortgage payment to a bank, the bank makes mortgage payments to him or her. Thus, the home owner becomes the mortgagee and the bank becomes the mortgagor. When both the home owners (his and her spouse), if any, are deceased, the home will go to the bank.

CHAPTER ELEVEN

11. Chapter eleven shows the features and definitions of terminologies used in this study. This is necessary because Real Estate industry has its own jargon or unique terminologies and moreover, a word may have more than one meaning. The definition in this chapter will help readers and users of this book to fully comprehend the context of certain words used in the text.

CHAPTER TWELVE

12. The conclusion and summary of the book is made succinct in this chapter. It shows a short synopsis of the text contents.

Tables And Figures

Table and Figures are used because of the questions asked when this book was presented to a group of real estate professionals. The questions that are asked are included. It presents or illustrates topics of tables and figures. The author agrees and promises that table(s) and figure(s) will be included in the book's text.

List of Tables

List of Figures

Contents

CHAPTER ONE
Preliminary

Chapter one illustrates this book, industry affiliations, target audience, main objective and author statements (partial autobiography). They show the ideas of the preliminary actions.

Introduction of the Book

Real Estate Transactions & Foreclosure Control book emphasizes the need for adequate knowledge and skills before involving oneself in a real estate transaction. Continuing, it provides significant information about home buying, selling and foreclosure that everyone needs to know and understand, especially those engaging in the real estate industry. Real estate professionals, non real-estate professionals (buyers and sellers) and new-arrivals in the industry will benefit from the evidence and advice in the book.

The Industry Affiliations

Research shows that Real Estate is the most significant industries in any society. As presented with a figure, real estate has affiliations with many other organizations. It also entertains a wide scope of assistance in the employment systems. Many employment opportunities develop from the network in the real estate industry and its affiliated entities. This is one reason why the industry has immeasurable influence on the economy of a country or any other society. Unfortunately, whenever the real estate industry of the country takes a downward turn, the economy of that country yields a similar lower turn.

The Target Audience

The target population for this study is anyone who benefits or wishes to benefit in any way or manner from the real estate industry. The contents of this book reflect what everyone needs to know about real estate transactions such as, real estate negotiations and foreclosures with repossessions. Research shows that, globally, most people live in homes or houses. Homes can be built with grass, leaves, mud, cement, bricks, metals, woods, stones and other materials. Nevertheless, each style when built is recognized as a home or shelter where people reside. If the concept of a home is held constant and since shelter is regarded as a primary need, it can be said that everyone lives in a home or is looking for a home to move in. In this case, everyone is a potential home buyer or home renter. It is easy to detect the role of real estate sellers, especially the Realtors. However, some of the most important actors in the industry are home buyers and home owners. Therefore, home buyers and home owners are the core and target audience of this book.

Main Objectives

Although, one purpose of writing this book is to help anyone who works in the real estate industry, the main objective is to assist, guide, educate and direct home buyers and owners as they profoundly keep the real estate industry flourishing and successful. Hence, this target population needs to know and understand the essential plans and actions needed before, during and after engaging in the purchase of any real estate property. Research shows that the costliest investments with most families are purchases of their homes. Thus, the main objective of this study is to structure the contents of this book in a way to offer home buyers and owners enough knowledge, skills and abilities to successfully handle their home purchases, home maintenances and home mortgages.

Author Statements

The author of this book is Dr. Frank M. Igah, Sr. I earned BS, MBA and Ph. D. degrees from universities in Dayton and Cincinnati, Ohio. My study of Finance with a focus in Real Estate is accomplished to a doctoral degree level. I have practiced as a Public Financial Analyst for more than thirty years and have been rewarded in many ways. I serve as a financial consultant to real estate professionals and buyers in different ways. I provide guidance and directions on how, what, when and where to make home purchases, sales, evaluations and negotiations before and after making real estate transactions. I write short-sale analyses that assist people to buy or sell homes with better contracts. My practice has lead me to participate in diverse and potent real estate transactions and meetings. The writing of short–sale documents and analyses have exposed me to many real estate lenders with whom I have held multiple meetings while exchanging skills and techniques. Further, I am a Licensed and Certified Mortgage Loan Officer. These credentials lead me to engage with businesses and other multiple lending institutions in multiple ways. The resulting factors are successful processing and making of mortgage loans. My public practices have assisted me in acquiring resilient skills, abilities, interests and experiences in the real estate transactions. Therefore, all these attributes, coupled with working as a certified mortgage loan officer and serving as professor in colleges afford me the unique qualifications to write a book of this nature.

Disclamation

Reading, understanding this book, Real Estate Transactions, Foreclosure Control, provides interesting, helpful and rewarding characteristics. However, the text does not cover all of the activities in the Real Estate industry. Like any other book, no reader should depend on it entirely. Therefore, buyers and sellers need to acquire other helpful knowledge through consultations and research whenever possible. For instance, this book does not comment on real estate bids and bidding practices. Furthermore, it does not comment on the serious side effects of real estate taxes nor does it contain vivid accounts of many performances of real estate companies. Also, the wrong calculations of Annual Percentage Rate (APR) and its negative as well as other influences on real estate mortgage financing, are not discussed in the book. However, if the readers of this book adopt and follow the contents carefully, they will achieve results that will help them save thousands of dollars and significantly minimize stress related issues, during their real estate transactions. Finally, I wish good luck to all my readers, buyers, sellers and other professionals in their real estate activities.

Affiliated Disciplines

It is significant to know that the mastery of real estate field requires a well informed knowledge to the real estate disciplines. When conducting an important research, it is necessary to examine all related issues which are significant to the works. Unfortunately, many home buyers do not have the essential knowledge in some of the needed fields related to the real estate industry. This is a reason why buyers need all the assistance they can receive, especially, since they must conform to the requirements of owning long-term mortgage loans. This book uncovers relevant facts, which will produce the necessary advice and assistance that can help home buyers and sellers achieve fundamental success. Basic knowledge in other real estate disciplines helps to promote real estate deals. The transactions in the real estate industry include comparisons and negotiations that are treated by other affiliated disciplines. These inter-related disciplines include economics, finance, marketing, elementary law, management and accounting. The diagram below, demonstrates how real estate industry ties together with other connected disciplines.

Affiliated Disciplines Contributing to the Real Estates Studies

STATISTICAL FACTS

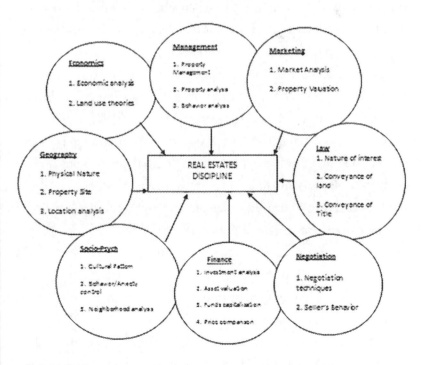

(Igah, St. 2013).

CHAPTER TWO
Real Estate
Mortgage Transactions

Mortgage Loan

This book is written to assist people in promoting sales and purchases of homes or houses and to enhance real estate marketability. A typical real estate purchase transactions include buyers, sellers, real estate agents or agencies and financiers. The financiers are the mortgage banks, commercial banks, mortgage brokers and other financial institutions, which are able and willing to engage in real estate mortgage financing. In most cases, realtors represent sellers. Most of the mortgage banks and financial institutions work with mortgage brokers who interview buyers and the borrowers. A mortgage company or broker interviews the clients or initiates the loan requests and completes the loan application forms along with other affiliated documents before sending all documents to a suitable financier. All decisions about loans, other types of funding, denials, approvals and pre-approvals are made by the mortgage financiers that supply the funds. It will be very helpful for realtors, sellers and buyers to have and retain the basic information that will help mortgage brokers to approve loan requests. A lender who approves a purchase loan, collects the monthly mortgage payments.

After a real estate deal is closed, the realtor earns commission, the broker retains the origination fees and the buyer pays the sale proceeds. Moreover, the buyer acquires a new property and the mortgage loan. Sometimes, purchases are fully paid while other times, they are paid in installments for a period of up to thirty years or more. Although, different persons and entities are involved in the real estate industry, this book may be of extra benefit to buyers because they carry the biggest burden in the success or failure of the market. Most of the burden that a buyer receives concerns the monthly payments of the acquired real estate mortgage loans. A real estate purchasing contract is complete after all participants receive their necessary payments. Subsequently, the buyer becomes the borrower and the mortgagee. The binding factor is between the borrower and the lender. Therefore, the borrower, who has received a mortgage payment, the buyer (borrower) and the lender (financier) continue with the payment bonds to them together for about thirty years or more. However, it is good to note that whenever the borrower makes a monthly payment, the lender earns a monetary reward called interest. The home mortgage borrower, if well maintained, receives equity or rewards constantly.

Recommendation

It is highly recommended that a buyer ready to consummate a real estate deal should:

- Acquire the services of a qualified financial professional.
- Hire a professional realtor to assist with the transactions.
- Read and understand the contents of this book before attempting to purchase a real estate or negotiate a mortgage loan.
- Properly evaluate his and her readiness (economically, financially and emotionally) prior to engaging in the purchase of a home, house or any loan.

- It is helpful to understand this book before buying a mortgage loan because the information obtained while reading the book will save the reader a good amount of money.

Further, the acquired information will also, provide buyers and sellers with the necessary tools to deal with multiple real estate issues. Sometimes, a buyer who obtains good credit figures and concerning his or her earning believes that he or she is able and ready to buy and own a home. Unfortunately, it is not quite true because the financial readiness may not be enough or satisfactory because a buyer could be mentally, emotionally, economically and spiritually deciding to purchase a home or another type of property. If the home buyer and other conditions are not adequate, the home or house purchases may be mismanaged. It is the intention of this book to equip buyers with the requisite knowledge they need before during and after they consummated a loan.

Apart from the discussions concerning real estate transactions, this book will deviate briefly to examine the effects of the existing depressed or recessed economy where the purchases of real estate properties are concerned. For instance, in the real estate market, both buyers and sellers are needed to initiate negotiations concerning selling and buying activities. Later, these activities will extend to mortgage lenders, appraisers, title companies and other affiliated persons or entities. It is a fact that the current economy in this country has greatly affects the real estate industry in tragic ways. Also, it is creating some adverse effects toward the transactions. These effects lead to stress, frustration, disappointment, foreclosure, repossession, pressure, homelessness and significant number of real estate buyers who have suffered them. In such condition, the buyers and sellers are forced to wait for the market to improve. The ramifications of forced waiting include anxiety and lack of trust in the real estate industry. Studies show that in any situation of trickled, recessed or depressed economy, the real estate industry is usually one of the first entities to feel the critical impact and the related hardships that follow. Subsequently, the entire market or industry takes a downward swing (Igah, Sr. 1983).

The Real Estate Industry

The importance of real estate industry in our society cannot be overly emphasized. The value of real estate constitutes a significant portion of the national wealth in the United States of America (USA) and the global markets. In every country, substantial people are directly or indirectly engaged in the real estate industry. When the real estate markets flourish, the estate buyers will start seeing good living and mortgage equities.

The high deficit and depressed economy, along with other erupting negative conditions have caused severe damages that include massive unemployment, multiple lay-offs, foreclosures, home repossessions, life-style changes, acute poverty, high homelessness, avoidable deaths, suicides, abnormal frustrations and untold hardships. Essentially, people of all age groups and cultures including singles, couples, children, teenagers, youth, adults, working- classes and retired persons are adversely affected.

Significance and Justification

Below is a short list of the reasons why this book is significance and justice.

1. This book emphasizes the positive and negative relationships in the buying and selling of any real estate property. Nowadays, all people, with the exception of some homeless persons, reside in a home or an apartment building. Accordingly, each person is a potential home or house buyer. Reading and understanding how to apply this book will help a person to save millions of costly mistakes such as real money, time and effort. Undoubtedly, the savings will be beneficial to the real estate industry and the economy of this country.

2. This is a unique book that portrays systematic and contemporary work in the real estate industry. Thereby, developing and maintaining the life of real estate industry.

3. Successful selling and buying of real estate and the increased marketability, produce upward trend where many people are appropriated to become employed.

4. Real estate industry is gigantic and embraces different employment categories. Building supplies are made possible because the industry are endlessly promote to homes/houses for buying and selling activities. People who engage themselves in real estate activities include property purchasers, property buyers, real estate brokers, stock and bond brokers, mortgage brokers, sales representatives, building contractors, property builders, property developers, government licensed or certified financiers, appraisers, surveyors, mortgage lenders, accountants, insurance companies, real estate lawyers, government personnel, building construction and maintenance workers, scientific and technological organizations, research teams and other industries that help sustain the

real estate industry in many was. The information in this book will assist real estate buyers, sellers and financiers to consummate their transactions smoothly and successfully.

Real Estate Purchase Contract

A buyer ready to purchase a property, makes an offer and requests to receive a purchase contract. Subsequently, the representative of the seller (in most cases, a trained realtor) will produce a complete property purchase contract. This contract is presented to the buyer for him to read, understood and sign. A real estate agreement is binding and the buyer must read and understand the contents of the documents before signing. The purchaser needs to take note of the agreement requirements such as allowable number of days for financing and closing the deal. If any item on the contract is unrealistic, the purchaser must decline the signing of the document and request an adjustment or more clarification. Next, a buyer takes a well executed purchase contract to a financier (a mortgage broker) and requests for a mortgage loan.

A reasonable purchase contract contains about twelve written paragraphs.

The headings are as follows.

1. Offer.
2. Price.
3. Deed.
4. Title Insurance.
5. Taxes.
6. Sellers or Representations.
7. Possession.
8. Damage to Building, if any.

9. Acceptance Closing.
10. Earnest Money Default.
11. General Provisions.
12. Inspections and Others.

An acceptable copy of a typical "Real Estate Purchase Contract" without an "Inspection Addendum" is included in the next few pages for the reader to familiarize with the required documents for real estate purchases. Here are the purchase documents.

Contract to Purchase Real Estate
(Mainly with a few changes, with Dayton
Board of Realtors, 2000)

**If the provisions are not understood, other
legal advice should be obtained.**

_____ Date: _____

(CITY)   **(STATE)**

1. **Offer.** The undersigned Purchaser offers to buy through

_____   _____,

Broker(s), on the terms and conditions set forth below, the real property (the "property") located in _____ (City/Township) _____ County of _____, State of _____described as follows:

The property shall include the land, appurtenant rights, privileges and easements, and all buildings, improvements and fixtures, including, but not limited to, such of the following as are now on the property: all electrical, heating, plumbing and bathroom fixtures; all window and door shades, blinds, awnings and screens; storm windows and doors; television antennae; curtain rods; garage door opener and control(s); all landscaping; and any personal property item listed above are owned by seller and will be free and clear of liens and security interest at the closing.

2. **Price.** The Purchaser agrees to pay for the property the sum of $_____, payable in cash at closing. Purchaser's obligations under this contract are conditioned upon Purchaser's ability to obtain prior to closing a mortgage loan of $_____ (conventional) (FHA) (VA) at rates and terms generally prevailing in the area.

(CITY)   **(STATE)**

Mortgage discount points/origination fees/prepaid items permitted by Lender/Purchaser's closing costs not to exceed _____are to be paid by Seller. Seller shall have the option to cancel this Contract if Purchaser fails to either (a) make a complete mortgage loan application including ordering an appraisal, within days after the date of acceptance of this offer or (b) obtain mortgage loan approval within days after the date of acceptance of this offer.

3. **Deed.** Seller shall furnish a transferable and recordable general warranty deed conveying to Purchaser or nominee, a marketable title to the property (as determined with reference to the _____State Bar Association Standards of Title Examination) with dower rights, if any, released, free and clear of all liens, rights to take liens and encumbrances whatsoever, except (a) legal highways, (b) any mortgage assumed by Purchaser, (c) all installments of taxes and assessments becoming due and payable at closing, (d)

rights of tenants in possession, (e) zoning and other laws and (f) easements and restrictions of record which would not prevent Purchaser from using the property for the following purpose: if title to all or part of the Property is unmarketable or is subject to matters not expected as provided above, Seller at Seller's sole cost shall cure any title defects and/or remove such matters within 10 days after receipt of written notice from Purchaser and if necessary the closing date may be extended to permit Seller the full 10 days to clear title.

4. **Title Insurance.** Purchasers are encouraged to inquire about the benefits of title insurance from the closing agent or other title insurance provider. A lender's policy of title insurance does not provide protection to the purchaser. It is recommended that purchasers obtain an owner's policy of title insurance to insure their own interests.

5. **Taxes.** At closing, Seller shall pay or credit to the purchase price (a) all real estate taxes and assessments, including penalties and interest, which became due and payable prior to the closing, (b) a pro rata share, calculated as of the closing date in the manner set forth below, of the taxes and assessments becoming due and payable after the closing and (c) the amount of any agricultural tax savings accrued as of the closing date which would be subject to recoupment if the property were converted to a non-agricultural use (whether or not such conversion actually occurs), unless Purchaser has indicated in paragraph 3 that Purchaser is acquiring the property for agricultural purposes. In whichever County the Property is located the tax proration shall be made in accordance with the County's "short proration" method, in which

Seller's share is based upon the number of days from the date immediately preceding semiannual installment to the date of closing. If the Property is located outside the _____ County, the tax proration shall be made in accordance with (check one); _____the County's "short proration" method or the _____ "long proration" method, in which Seller's share is based upon the taxes and assessments which are a lien for the year of closing. (If neither method is checked, the short proration shall apply). If the short proration method is used, any special assessments which are payable in a single annual installment shall nevertheless be prorated on the long proration method. All proration shall be based upon the most recent available tax rates, assessments and valuations.

6. **Sellers Representations.** Seller represents that those signing this contract constitute all of the owners of the title to the Property, together with their respective spouses. Seller further represents that with respect to the Property (a) no orders of any public authority are pending, (b) no work has been performed or improvement constructed that may result in future assessments, (c) no notice has been received from any public agency with respect to condemnation or appropriation, change in zoning, proposed future assessments, corrections of conditions or other similar matters and (d) to the best of Seller's knowledge, no toxic, explosive or other hazardous substances having been stored, disposed of, concealed within or released on or from the Property and no other adverse environmental conditions affect the Property. These representations shall survive the closing.

7. **Possession.** Rentals, interest on any assumed mortgages, water, other utility bills and any current operating expenses shall be prorated as of the date of closing. If the Property is owner-occupied, the possession will be given _____days after closing at ___a.m. or p.m. The utilities shall not be prorated as above but paid for by seller until delivery of the possession. Seller shall be responsible to Purchaser for any damages resulting from the Seller's failure to deliver possession on the due date.

8. **Damage to Buildings.** If any building or other improvements receive substantial damage(s) prior to the closing time, purchaser shall have the following options (a) to proceed with the closing and receive the proceeds of any insurance payable in connection therewith or (b) to terminate this Contract. Seller shall keep the Property adequately insured against fire and extended coverage perils prior to closing. Seller maintains the Property in its present condition until delivery of possession.

9. **Acceptance Closing.** This offer shall remain open for acceptance until _____ (Date), at 11:59 p.m. The closing for delivery of the deed and payment of the balance of the purchase price shall be held on or before_____(Date) at a time and place mutually agreed upon by seller and purchaser. In the event of failure of both parties to agree, the closing shall be held on the last day designated in this paragraph and the Selling Broker shall designate the time and place of closing.

10. **Earnest Money Default.** Upon presentation of this offer, Purchaser has delivered to _____, (Broker) the sum of _____as earnest money to be (1) deposited in the

Broker's trust account promptly after acceptance of this offer or (2) returned to Purchaser upon request if this offer is not accepted. The earnest money shall be paid to Purchaser or applied on the purchase price at closing. If the closing does not occur because of Seller's default or because any condition of this contract is not satisfied or waived, Purchaser shall be entitled to the earnest money. The parties acknowledge, however, that the Broker will not make a determination as to which party is entitled to the earnest money. Instead, the Broker shall release the earnest money from the trust account only (a) in accordance with the joint written instructions of Seller and Purchaser or (b) in accordance with the following procedure: if the closing does not occur for any reason(including the default of either party), the Broker holding the earnest money may notify Seller in writing that the earnest money will be returned to Purchaser unless Seller makes a written demand for the earnest money within 20 days after the date of the Broker's notice. If the Broker does not receive a written demand from Seller within 20-day period, the Broker shall return the earnest money to Purchaser. If a written demand is received by the Broker within 20-day period, the Broker shall retain the earnest money until (i) Seller and Purchaser have settled the dispute; (ii) disposition has been ordered by a final court order; or (iii) the Broker deposits the earnest money with the court pursuant to applicable court procedures. Payment or refund of the earnest money shall not prejudice the rights of the Broker(s) or the non-defaulting party in action for damages or specific performance against the defaulting party.

11. General Provisions. Upon acceptance, this offer shall become a complete agreement binding upon and inuring to the benefit of Purchaser and Seller and their respective heirs, personal representatives, successors and assigns and shall be deemed to contain all the terms and conditions agreed upon, there being no oral conditions, representations, warranties or agreements. Any subsequent conditions, representations warranties or agreements shall not be valid and binding upon the parties unless in writing signed by both parties. Purchaser has examined the Property and, except as otherwise provided in this Contract, is purchasing it "as is" in its present condition, relying upon such examination as to the condition, size, utility and zoning of the Property. Time is of the essence of all provisions of this Contract. Any word used in this Contract shall be construed to mean either singular as indicated by the number of signatures below.

Inspection and Other Addenda: The following addenda and attachments are attached to and shall be considered an integral part of this Contract:

_____Inspection Addendum; _____Land Contract Addendum; _____Other (Describe)

WITNESS: _____ **Purchase:** _____

_____ **Purchaser:** _____

MAKE DEED TO (PRINT): _____

Address: _____

ACCEPTANCE   Date: _____

The undersigned Seller (_____) accepts the foregoing offer: or (_____) counteroffer according to the initialed changes set forth above or in the attached Addenda, which offer or counteroffer shall remain open for acceptance until_____ at 11: 59 p.m.

WITNESS: _____ **Seller** _____

Not accepted at this time. Thank you for your offer.

Seller: _____ **P r i n t :** _____

Seller: _____ **P r i n t :** _____

Deposit Receipt

Receipt is acknowledged of _____earnest money to be deposited in the undersigned Broker's trust account upon acceptance of this offer and to be applied as provided in paragraph 10 above.

F i r m _____ **By (Agent)** _____ **REALTOR**

P h o n e: _____

CHAPTER THREE
Home Ownership

The Need for a Home

A core of this book is to assist households, home buyers, sellers and other real estate professionals to accomplish their business goals

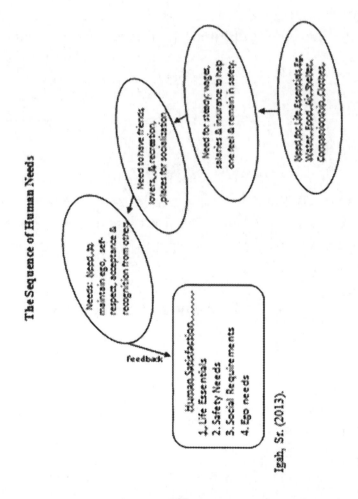

more efficiently. Generally, people purchase life necessities such as shelter, food and medicine before buying pleasurable or fanciful goods such as automobiles, boats or leisure trips. Life necessities are classified as physiological needs, real estate properties, shelters or homes. Also, some disciplines, such as Business and Psychology, refer to physiological needs as primary needs. Requiring a primary need is required before a secondary need. The value of a primary need is researched by Maslow, McClelland and Alderfer with Certo, 2003.

Every person has a need to reside somewhere. Today, most people prefer to own homes, if they have enough finances to purchase their essential homes. In fact, home renters (tenants) are sometimes referred to as temporary buyers or home owners without equity. If a tenant pays rent in a given month, the same tenant owns the use of the entire space for that same month. This is particularly beneficial to tenants of single-family homes. Indeed, for reasons of safety and essential characteristics, human beings have their own homes. History teaches us that before the age of civilization, ancient men cherished the idea of having their own homes. The early humans built homes with wild leaves and grasses. Later, their homes are built in underground rocks (caves). Carvings or cave homes are safer and more protected from wild animals and inclement weathers than the homes built with leaves and grasses (Mcgowan & Hester, Jr., 1962).

Due to high-tech modern technologies, men no longer live in caves. They currently build homes with mud blocks, bricks, sticks, cement and /or stones. The efficacy in home building concept, presents a need for land ownership, farming and building homes. In 1776, all land in the USA belonged to the Federal government. Citizens qualify for portions and titles of land that the government presents to them. The history of most land titles in the United States of America (USA) can be traced to a grant or patent from the current Federal government. Today, the USA owns more land than she did centuries ago. Therefore, to enable families to build their homes and plant their crops on the farm land, the government must do something to provide more land for people to create the activities in homes and farm land. Subsequently, the various "treaties," "ordinances" and "Land Acts" of the government assist to bring about various land acquisitions and annexations to the people. As these need occur, more states are created and people are more able to acquire enough land titles to build homes and establish settlements, hence, the importance of land is shown in the table below (Igah, Sr., 1983).

Federal Land Agreements

Promulgation Declaration Date Accomplishments

Land Ordinance	October 10, 1780	Annexation of Western lands between the Alleghenies and the Mississippi.
Treaty of Paris	1783	Granted US all territory North latitude east of Mississippi.
Land Ordinance	May 20, 1785	Adapted a rectangular system of Surveys; Allowed for the sales of the Public land of the United States.
NW Land Ordinance	July 13, 1787	Established a precedent that an individual's land from the government involved the entire transfer of ownership of the soil. At death, an individual's estate passes to his rightful family.

Land Act	1800	Introduced disposition of land through the officers called "registers" who would direct to see that land was transferred for sale at the public auction and at the offices
Purchase Agreement "Land Acquisition"	1803	Paid $ 27,267,621 to France for the purchase of Louisiana and all land in the Western drainage basin of the Mississippi River. The country's area practically doubled with this purchase.
Purchase Agreement "Land Acquisition"	1819	The Florida State (land space) was purchased from Spain for $6,589,768.
Establishment "Land Claim"	1846	More land was claimed from England for dispute settlement. The land was called the Oregon Territory and was used to create the States of Oregon, Washington and Idaho.
Land Treaty Purchase Agreement	1848	Purchase of the "Mexican Territory" for $15,000,000. This territory was used to create the States of California, Nevada, Utah, parts of Colorado, Arizona and New Mexico
Land Settlement "Land Acquisition"	1853	Purchase of Southern boundary from Mexico through the "Gadsden Purchase."
Purchase Agreement "Land Acquisition"	1867	Purchase of Alaska from Russia for $7,200,000.

SOURCE: (Igah, 1983).

A real estate property such as a home, factory, farm land, office or government building may be the most valuable asset for the person who owns it, especially, a middle class family. Land ownership is basic and an expensive of human ambition. Hence, land disputes are blamed for many wars and other cultural conflicts. Also, people buy and sell vacant lands and landed properties. These practices help give birth to the real estate industry. Therefore, to fully understand real estate history one must review the tables of Federal Land Agreements, Significance of the Real Estate Industry with land ownership and the Various Stages of Human Growth and Civilization.

Although it is ambitious and prestigious to own a home, it is also clear that a home is not merely a luxury, but also a necessity. For instance, people need to take refuge inside homes to survive extreme weather and protect poor conditions from wild animals. A person who intends to buy a home needs genuine support and encouragement as it is the nature of humans to live in their houses/homes. Further, as people and civilization continue to develop, so are ways to make a home safer and more luxurious. Very often, some persons refer to their homes as bunks, cabins, castles, huts and mansions.

The real estate industry grows rapidly, partly because of the constant increase in the number of real estate professionals. As a result, efforts are made to carry out studies that concern the industry. Evidently, education in real estate fields, such as Law, Appraisal, Administration and Finance, are potent disciplines studied in schools, universities and training institutions. Studies show that the endings of wars precipitate rapid boom periods and better effectiveness in the real estate industry. The prosperity or boom leads to the "American Dream," which in turn, improves the economy in the country.

Subsequently, the Federal and local governments establish measures that encourage people to continue to buy homes and fulfill their "American Dream." Studies show that the Asian wars (including Vietnam) have resulted in the returning soldiers flashing in the real estate market boom, which existed until 1969. Moreover, an increase in government spending hastened or hurried the use of Federal Housing Administration (FHA) and Veteran Administration (VA) mortgage programs. These programs help to provide better excess to the ex-service citizens to consummate home financing. Undoubtedly, the "boom periods" of the real estate industry contribute extensively to the size, wealth, fame and strength of this country. In fact, to discuss success in real estate industry is to give credit to rapid boom periods.

The table below shows the economic boom periods. Some readers may be able to look at the dates below and recall the booms in the economy of this country. Therefore, to a large degree, events in real estate industry help to influence the economy of the country.

Summary of Boom Periods with Causes and Duration

DESCRIPTION	DATE	CAUSES	DURATION
First Boom Period	between 1923 & 1929	World War I	Seven Years
Second Boom Period	between 1947 & 1957	World War II	Eleven Years
Third Boom Period	between 1964 & 1969	Vietnam War	Five Years
Fourth Boom Period	between 2003 & 2008	Sub-Prime Programs & Federal Spending	Six Years

(Igah, Sr. Partial, Real Estate Research, 1983)

Proportion of Real Estate Properties with Diagram

The study of real estate transactions shows that single to four family homes are the most important and popular properties in the industry because they constitute more than half of the entire real estate properties. The remainder include Farm Properties, Commercial Estates and multi-family (five and above) homes. The diagram below shows the type of properties in the real estate industry and the approximate proportion or size of each type.

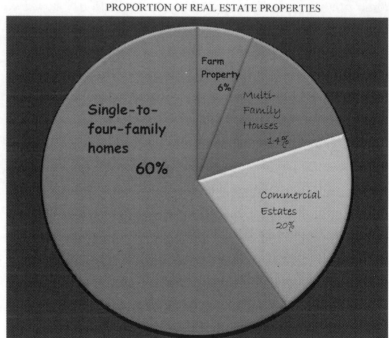

PROPORTION OF REAL ESTATE PROPERTIES

SOURCE: Primarily adopted from Igah, Sr. (1983).

The Distribution of the Diagram Above

1. Farm Properties - cover six per cent of the real estate industry.
2. Commercial Estates - cover twenty per cent of the real estate industry.

3. Multi-Family Dwellings - cover fourteen per cent of the real estate industry.

4. Single-to-four-family homes - cover sixty per cent of the real estate industry.

Advantages of Single Family Homes

Single family houses are private housing. They are the most purchased and most popular type of private housing. It is also widely believed that the locations of single family houses are instrumental to defining various cultures and classes in society. Again, people will very often classify single- family homes or communities as upper-upper class, upper class, upper middle class, middle class, middle lower class, lower class and lower-lower class. Culture, consciously and unconsciously, partitions society in many ways. Single family homes located on the country-side reflect the preference or favorite of the wealthy upper-class citizens, while the suburban single family homes are often categorized as middle-class life. The middle-lower class citizens usually settle in condominiums or town houses which classify as private housing. The lower class citizens mostly settle in the most crowded parts of the urban and often rent apartment houses.

Multiple family homes, Condominiums, town houses and Commercial Estates are usually attached to one another and share a common wall. One of the most common differences between these habitats and ordinary apartments is that, very often, the occupants of condominiums or town houses are purchasers of their units while the tenants of apartment complexes are renters. Ordinarily, at the end of each month, apartment or home renters (tenants) pay rents to their landlords or landladies, while the single home purchasers pay mortgages to their financiers. Studies show that predominantly American citizens continue to reside in single-family properties which require mortgage payments. Single homes afford the option to enjoy better comfort, privacy, prestige, equity and investment for the homes. Therefore, it is more likely that most families would prefer to own their homes.

Mortgage and Rent Compared

Some single homes are rented and tenants observe rules, regulations or policies that concern lodging. In this case, tenants of single-family homes enjoy the advantages of private single homes, except the equity in the homes which go to the home owner. On the other hand, some people purchase apartments as homes and pay monthly payments. In fact, a few years ago, the author purchased six units of an apartment building and stayed in the complex. He combined two (adjacent) units and paid monthly mortgages. Actually, mortgage payments are high insurance payments which are much higher than house rents. Generally, when a single-family home and an apartment house are compared, the single-family home seems to have much more spacious and other advantages than an apartment unit.

Mortgage Family Homes

Some of them are as follows:
Private Entrance

Commonly, people who live in apartment buildings enter their homes through the same entrance doors. This arrangement can invade the privacy of other tenants who live in the building. The activities of tenants upon entering the buildings are exposed to other tenants and guests in the buildings. A single family home has private entrances that isolate the activities in the homes. Occasionally, private entrances afford home owner's guests in the home, the opportunity to enter and exit the property unnoticed by others. Ordinarily, people value or welcome the concept of privacy for residents and their guests.

Free Standing

In all cases, single-family homes stay alone, hence they are called single-family houses or homes. Standing alone means that the home/ house is not detached to any other building. Therefore, a home owner does not share a compound with a neighbor. Usually, a single-home has a separate driveway with alley. An uninvited guest in the compound is an intruder. A home owner may install a fence around the home to provide more privacy. Examples of free standing single-family homes with private entrances are shown below.

Two-Level Homes with Private Entrances and Detached Garages

Front and Back Yards

A single family home has front and back yards that are exclusively unique for the home. Yards enhance the beauty and value of the homes. Fenced yards afford the residents of a home luxury, safety, privacy, recreation and other activities. Also, a home owner has the privilege of building or installing a storage unit on his or her back yard. The private driveway and vehicle garage provide privacy and security for the automobile. On the contrary, the yard, driveway and /or vehicle garage of an apartment building is shared by all tenants residing in the building.

Play Ground Space

A single-family home affords the home owner and family members are a comfortable play-ground for physical activities, such as basket ball, tennis, swimming, jogging and soccer. The children of the home enjoy supervised play time and engage in various activities which are of interest to them. On the other hand, a tenant in an apartment building may not install fitness and play ground equipment for children or adults because the property belongs to the house owner (landlord or landlady). Any equipment must be approved by the home owner. Further, the equipment may very likely be shared by other tenants in the building.

Open Space

A single-family home contains open spaces which gives the home owner excellent opportunities to add extra rooms. Obtaining a county or city housing reconstruction permit affords the home owner an opportunity to build additions such as pet shelter, extra rooms and a relaxation state. This arrangement differs with apartment buildings where tenants are required to obtain written permission from the owner before installing any material or equipment.

Surrounding Geography

The geography surrounding a property helps to improve health and wellness in the community. Many home owners upgrade their landscapes by planting trees, shrubs and flowers around their homes and in their yards. As a result, the compound is beautified with rich fresh shrubs and natural fragrances from the green environment. Some home owners enjoy the outdoor views from their balconies and decks. Apart from a normal home landscape, some shrubs are planted to control erosion. Multiple homes in the city have healthy landscapes that not only serve for aesthetic views but also to help prevent flood, erosion and other potential natural disasters.

Residing in a Low Density Area

Generally, single-family homes in the neighborhoods are regarded as low density areas, due to low crime rates. A reason for this low crime rate, results from active neighborhood watch programs. It is said that usually, criminal activities occur in high density areas due to congestion of a sometimes lawless population. Criminal activities in the high density areas are relatively more difficult to assess because of increased felonious activities. Low density areas are less likely to experience crimes such as thefts, arsons and rape. Consequently, home owners in low density areas enjoy better levels of peace.

Out of Way Location

Apartment units are separated by single walls that are, customarily, not noise proof from other tenants in the building. Consequently, tenants can be disturbed by noise coming from neighboring units. Examples of such troubling noises are, squeaking sounds, music, television programs, conversation, telephone words and argument voices. Many of these apartments are located in high density neighborhoods of the city. On the other hand, single-family homes are usually in out of the way locations. These homes are built away from the city noise and traffic pathways.

Prestige and Satisfaction

Home owners enjoy, owning their homes, better privacies, excellent credit ratings, positive societal recognition and other personal satisfactions. Renters of single-family homes may enjoy some of the above attributes. It is prestigious and impressive for people to own the houses they live. Borrowers and purchases with high credit ratings have fewer purchasing issues when they seek to own large assets such as automobiles or real estate properties.

Ownership of Valuable Asset

Generally, the value of an asset depreciates over the years. However, properly maintained homes may appreciate in value over time. Therefore, the equity of home owners increases yearly. For example, well maintained homes may sell double of purchased price fifty years ago. It is imperative that people understand the fundamental principles of investments. It is reassuring to own an asset that will appreciate in value and serve as collateral for future new investment. For example, a home owner is likely to qualify for a car loan faster than a home renter. A home yields equity that affords the home owner the opportunity to make significant investment that yields a gainful Return on Investment (ROI). Finally, the home owner will attain a profitable future resale the amount for the same property.

Choosing a Home

A question of many people ask if it is better to choose a potential property to purchase before making sure that one qualifies for the rating ratios and closing costs of the property? The answer to this question is a resounding yes. It is better for buyers to select a property of choice, in their minds, before checking to know if they qualify with the rating ratios and closing costs. Further, it is equally important to select the location or site the buyer may prefer for the closing cost. It is imperative to know that ratio percentages fall within property variables such as: value, maintenance and amenities present in the purchase price of the property. Purchase price depends on the appraisal value of the classification, size and location of the property. A big luxurious fanciful home that sits in a safer neighborhood will attract higher purchase price than an identical property that sits in a less safe location. However, it is necessary for potential property buyers to perform general evaluation of their financial and credit standings before attempting to physically select properties to purchase. Finally, buyers need to make sure that their credit scores, closing funds and down payment funds are ready, prior to engaging in any type of property negotiations.

Property buyers, engaging in real estate transactions must be very careful consummating the transactions because, an inadvertent mistake is capable of creating a long term misfortune for them. For instance, a person who suffers from grand mal seizure may no longer need a house with many steps in it, due to safety purposes. Different types of single-family dwellings are defined below.

- **Ranch house:** A ranch house has all rooms on one floor. Usually there are no steps in the house, except to access a basement. A person, who has qualifying disability and prefers to live in a ranch home with a basement, will need to make adjustments such as an elevator, in order to accommodate the presenting disability.
- **Two level house:** A two-level house has an upstairs. It has steps which provide smoother flexibility to access the upper level section of the house.
- **Three-level house:** A three-level house has a set of stairs. Generally, it has two floors on top of the first floor. In actuality, it has much more stairs than a two level house in order to provide access to the second and third floor levels of the house. Of course, a home owner may decide to contain elevators.
- **Town house:** A town house is built on two levels. The second floor is built on top of the first floor. A town house comes with multiple steps.
- **Duplex:** A duplex is a building for two separate occupants. It is designed like two single family homes that are joined together. Some duplexes are built in the form of ranch houses while others are built to have levels. Duplexes are with one level or two levels and can either have fewer or more stairs.

- **Condominium:** A condominium has three or more separate occupants. It is built like two or more duplexes joined together. Apart from the homes on the first floor, the rest have multiple steps or elevators.

These choices are open to a buyer who must make genuine efforts to visit and evaluate every house or home, including choosing the ideal location. After a purchaser gives a written offer and deposits the earnest money, it becomes too late to point out any defect that exists in the house. Any noticeable defect needs to be added to the total price before making the final offer. The earnest money from the purchaser is usually non refundable if an offer and acceptance on the property have taken place between purchaser and the real estate seller.

Home Investment

Investment is the capital on a valuable asset, which has a calculated maximum rate of future returns, in the risk category. As mentioned before, it is generally believed that the largest investment that most families make is the purchase of their homes. A major reason for this is because the purchase of a home consumes most of the finances in a family budget, both in the present and in the future. This valuable asset will need genuine attention in the areas of maintenance and future monthly payments. The analysis of investments include some of the following.

Classes of Business and Financial Risks

Uncertainties – These are actions that may inadvertently happen to homes.

Examples include foreclosing, repossession, fire, flood and other accidental damages.

Variability – These vary according to the presenting economy of the location. Examples of Variability include variable interest, real estate taxes and insurance rates. Debt tie down occurs when buyers are unable to purchase or finance their real estate assets.

A purchaser needs to remember that a highly maintained neighborhood enhances the resale value of a well maintained of home, thereby yielding high Return on Investment (ROI).

- **Expected Future Return:** This is the income from the investment, referred to as Return on Investment **(ROI).** The ROI is the expected future yields which a buyer hopes to realize from the home. Without the ROI, the real estate operation or purchase is regarded as speculation or consumption. An advantage in real estate property is that unlike many other assets, the property that is well maintained does not depreciate rather; it appreciates in value over the time. This means that the net equity from the home will serve as or contribute towards, the ROI of the investment.
- **Capital Expenditure:** This is used for the purchase of real estate assets. In this case, the capital expenditure is the home mortgage that has been paid up, presently being paid or will be paid in the future to acquire the home.
- **Valuable Asset:** This is the asset in which the investment of the buyer is made or being made. In this discussion, the valuable asset is the home purchased or being purchased.

Although, homes yield Return on Investment (ROI), the purchase of homes is not readily classified as an investment because it has the properties of investment and non-investment attached to it. Further, it is not basically true that a home owner builds future equity with every mortgage payment made because the equity may or may not mature due to continuing inherent risks that follow the investment. Mortgage equity is not an investment, it is forced savings. However, some levels of investments are involved if at a later date the house is able to sell at a higher amount than it was purchased. In this case, the net cash realized becomes the ROI for the home owner, which can be reinvested (Amling, 1981).

A house appreciates in value in many instances and sells for more than it was previously purchased. However, a good rule of thumb is that the appreciation value is not likely to happen during the time of low economic activities such as trickle recession or depression in the country. A potential home buyer must first, calculate his or her prospective rate of return towards the investment before making solid purchase plan. Another advantage a home owner has is, after some years, the purchaser may capitalize on the built up equity. Further, the owner does not have to wait long before taking advantage of some or all of the accumulated equity or Return on the Investment (ROI) to refinance the home. Refinancing a home may begin after five years of property ownership.

A home owner may obtain "cash-out" from the built up equity and use it to refinance or maintain the home. Also, the proceeds can be reinvested in other assets or securities that can yield comfortable ROI in less volatile and lower risk class neighborhood. When the home owner consummates these techniques, the home purchase becomes an accomplishment. This home owner attains future returns and safer capital growth. In this situation, the capital is the money spent to purchase the home. This also means that the mortgage payments are consistent. Therefore, all real estate capital expenditures, including unplanned purchases may not be called investments. However, based on the concept that the capital increases with each periodic payment, the outcome becomes an investment.

Facts that Concern Buying Homes

Real estate transactions can be complex hence, fundamental educational knowledge and practical skills are necessary factors that assist a person in making better and guided decisions before, during and after the purchase of a home or any other real estate property. These potent credentials are especially important during a trickled, recessed or depressed economy. Indeed, some buyers do not have the awareness and understanding that they need for successful purchase of homes. These essential factors are not legal requirements, however, they are necessary for completing transactions successfully. Below are tips to use while purchasing a real estate property.

(i)   A seller is more likely than not to be represented by a real estate agent. A real estate agent is a trained and experienced professional in the real estate field. Sometimes buyers are not represented by experts during real estate negotiation processes. A buyer, in most cases, is without adequate knowledge of real estate transactions.

(ii) The real estate agent assumes the position of the seller. The agent is expected to have more requisite knowledge and experience to properly guide the seller (client) towards making safer and more successful sale. Unfortunately, some well educated buyers do not believe that they need guidance in making better transactions.

(iii) Sometimes possession of knowledge (like college education) may lead a buyer to feel too confident while handling purchasing deals.

(iv) A buyer who proceeds to handle all the real estate purchasing transactions without engaging an expert in the field is more likely than not to make expensive mistakes, especially on the negotiating table. First, the buyer may make a careless or bogus offer and deposit an earnest money which may eventually be lost due to ineffective transaction.

(v) An offer and acceptance encourage the buyer to intensify more serious discussions that lead to finalize a mortgage loan arrangement with a mortgage lender. The lender may be a mortgage broker that represents mortgage lenders, commercial banks or other financial institutions. A lender working with a buyer has mortgage lending trainings, practical experiences and skills that are acquired in the field of services. In fact, mortgage brokers must be certified by the government. Also, they must attain required hours of continued education classes. In fact, real estate agents and the mortgage brokers (lenders) must successfully complete essential educational courses and the State Board Examination before practicing in the real estate field. The education and other attributes required to accomplish licensures afford participants unique and specialized knowledge to operate as real estate agents and lenders. Evidently, with all these in place, the clients will benefit effectively from real estate services.

(vi) It is apparent that both the real estate agent (who represents the seller) and the professional mortgage lender (who makes the money available to a borrower) are familiar with rules, skills, abilities, government regulations, bargaining and other short-cut techniques needed for the buying and selling of properties effectively. A property buyer, who reads and understands this book, will be able to eliminate significant negative stress or stressors and avoid poor contracting arrangements. In fact, a buyer may attain more formal education than a servicing agent and a lender. However, the same buyer may not have the necessary fundamental knowledge of the real estate field. For this reason, the buyer may lack special skills, knowledge, experiences and abilities required for making better purchase transactions in the real estate industry.

A vital achievement in understanding this handbook is to know that it can guide a buyer to navigate smoothly, through any type of real estate purchasing transactions including private, public and commercial deals. Regardless of whether the purchase of a property is for personal or commercial use, a buyer who reads and understands this book has the contemporary prerequisite knowledge needed to successfully complete a transaction.

A home buyer, who makes a mistake during the purchase of a home, may refinance the home; engage in better transactions and subsequently save a lot of money. In fact, depending on the levels of knowledge in real estate, a person reading this book may still not have enough real world experience; however, this book can serve as an essential eye opener. With this knowledge, a home buyer can now begin and ask effective questions, especially in a deal that involves more than one real estate agent. Also, the use of consultation is encouraged for both parties (buyer and seller) to consummate a deal properly. Consultants are qualified specialists in their field of practices, such as Financial Analyst and Accountants.

An example case could be the following: A buyer is interested in purchasing a new home. So, the home buyer obtains a real estate agent called "X." "X" finds a property agent "Y" lists for sale. The two agents, "X" and "Y," decide to work as a team to sell the property and share the commission. In such a case, agent "X" would act as if he or she represents the buyer. If the buyer leans towards the ideas of agent "X" and purchases the home that is suggested, when the property is sold, agent "Y" will serve as the payer to agent "X". Generally, a person owes allegiance to whoever issues his or her paychecks. Indeed, you may be making a serious mistake, when you permit a realtor to act as your agent in handling purchasing transactions that concerns a property listed for sale by another realtor. Understand that realtors sell properties together for profit. Therefore, they negotiate prices as high as possibly to share gainful commissions. However, a relator who fails to sell a property receives no commission or paycheck. Unfortunately, the buyer is the one paying for all the transaction costs and the commission. Now that real estate purchase transactions and techniques are being discussed, it may be beneficial to show a buyer some plans and actions that are necessary to acquire before requesting for mortgage loan financing.

CHAPTER FOUR
Plans And Actions "Before" Mortgage Financing

Mortgage in the context of real estate purchase is the house or property loan that a buyer acquires. The word mortgage means a loan and a pledge. Lenders usually ask for collateral to secure the loan they offer to a borrower. Therefore, a property buyer borrows money to buy a home or a house on the condition that the same home or house serves as a pledge to the lender in the form of collateral or security. Thus, the borrower becomes the mortgagor and the lender becomes the mortgagee. The outcome of a real estate purchase is that the buyer has a personal property not a real property. Mortgages are financed for any length of time comfortable to the mortgagor for ten, fifteen, thirty or more years, but most are financed for thirty years. If the buyer pays all maturing fees during the life of a mortgage loan, at the end of financed term (thirty more or less years), the property buyer receives a transfer of the legal title from the lender and becomes an owner of a real property.

As discussed earlier, a buyer needs to be aware of some essential facts and techniques before embarking on any mortgage financing arrangements. Factual data and techniques prepare a buyer ready for a trouble shooting and the manager's stress that are inevitable with mortgage financing deals. During the period of planning for a mortgage loan financing, if any significant item is missing or incomplete on a document, the buyer needs to spend quality time to study and make all necessary corrections that may exist. Applicable ingredients for planning a mortgage loan financing include risks, credit reports, funds, income, debt ratios, credit judgment and personal records of the purchaser.

Mortgage Risk Analysis "Before" Financing

Real estate purchasers need to calculate all conceivable risks involved in the financing of the mortgage they plan to acquire. The foremost risks are classified as business and financial risks.

Business Risk

A home owner does not have much of business risk to worry about except if the home is a rental property. If so, planning and administering of the rental transactions need to be thorough. For instance, there may be months when a tenant will default on rent payments, the house is vacant or needs enormous renovations. A technique that helps property owners entice people to rent a property on a timely manner is to offer renters monetary rent discounts (10% to 15%) or ask potential tenants to skip rent payment for some time. It is advantageous for a renter to prepare and circulate a rental lease agreement that includes sixty days moving out notice, as it gives the property owner reasonable time to arrange for another tenant, thereby minimizing vacancy risks. Vacancy risks include loss of rents, insurances, property taxes and property vandalisms. If these adverse vacancy factors are not controlled, the business risks of the landlord or renter will expand.

Financial Risk

An appropriate financial plan works to control or mitigate the financial risks that may result from an unforeseen occurrence.

When a buyer defaults on the mortgage payments, the lender forecloses the mortgage contract. Henceforth, the lender proceeds to repossess the property. The property buyer or landlord loses all the capital investments previously made on the property. This type of situation happens multiple times, especially during the periods of depression and mismanagement economy in a country. A home or house buyer needs to know these facts before making a solid decision to purchase. Generally, the thought of business or financial risks does not stop many people from buying real estate because the risks are mostly intangible. More and more, people prefer to remain optimistic and hope to improve their future business and financial conditions. However, the idea of conquering potential risks should be taken seriously. Nevertheless, well maintained plan of action, will help to defeat future financial risks.

Credit Data Analysis "Before" Financing

To determine the readiness of a would-be purchaser engaging in a financing deal, the purchaser must obtain and examine his or her credit reports. A person's credit reports show credit scores, public records and other necessary personal matters. A home purchaser determines his/her credit score policy at an acceptable range in points (400 to 800). The recommended average credit score derived from the three most trusted credit score institutions (Equifax, Transunion and Experian) range from 600 to 650 points. Sometimes, lenders accept 580 points or the median score. Poor credit reports depreciate the character of its owner. Factors that include rent mortgage and auto mismanaged payments, can cause the denial of a loan requested by a purchaser. Further, public records and other unfavorable items such as negative court or police reports may draw back and discredit a person from receiving favorable loan amount.

Unsatisfied Court Judgment

A home buyer, who does not satisfy a guilty verdict from a court action has an unsatisfied court action. Under this condition, the loan request of this home buyer will be deferred until the buyer presents a release (court document) that shows a compromising deal. In the event that the purchaser has a court default, he or she should purchase from the court and obtain a clear paper.

Outstanding Court Case

If a real estate purchaser and loan applicant are defendants in an outstanding court case, both the real estate loan and the purchasing activities will be put on hold pending adjudication. However, if the loan applicant is the plaintiff, the processing of the loan and purchasing of the property will be processed, nevertheless, the potential proceeds from the case will not be an income for the plaintiff.

Default Student Loan

Defaulting on student loans is a serious issue, which often involves the government because the federal government makes and guarantees student loans. Generally, if a purchaser is in default of a student loan, the real estate institution will deny the loan application. In this situation, the purchaser can use any of the three methods listed below to solve the problem before applying for a mortgage loan financing.

(a) The home purchaser could make student loan payments with installment bases as arranged with the student loan collector. Later, this purchaser may release payment receipt(s) to the real estate lender.

(b) The purchaser could negotiate and defer the loan to a future date and submit the deferring document to the real estate lender.

(c) The purchaser could pay off the loan and submit the court receipt to the real estate lender.

Default Credits

Therefore, a loan applicant may negotiate feasible monthly payments, obtain receipts and send them to the money lender. If the monthly payment is given, the negotiation must begin as soon as possible. The credit report needs to show "paying as agreed" before applying for a real estate loan. The applicant may submit the "paying as agreed" document along with the loan application. However, it should be noted that a newly added debt increases the debt ratio of the applicant.

Trade Accounts

A mortgage loan applicant maintains a minimum of three trade accounts prior to applying for the loan. These trade accounts can be with any whole sale or retail business organization.

Recent Bankruptcy or Foreclosure

A real estate loan applicant with bankruptcy will be rejected. Also, the loan applicant must wait for a minimum of three to five years before applying for a home purchase loan. In the case of a bankruptcy, the waiting period begins to count from the day of a bankruptcy discharge and not the day that the bankruptcy was filed in the court.

The best way for a buyer to detect an adverse issue is to obtain their credit report and read under the credit report headings called "Summary of Derogatory Items" and "Public Records." The loan and home purchase will suffer a short delay while waiting to repair the presenting issues. It is imperative to remain calm and consult with appropriate resources such as reading this book again, credit repair agencies and other potent real estate business.

Required Funds "Before" Financing

Prior to consulting a lender, a home buyer needs to check for the availability of funds that will help with the consummation of mortgage financing. Three financial requirements needed to complete the mortgage loans are down payment, appraisal fee and closing cost. The occurrences concerning acute economic recession in this country (USA) help to bring about the best home mortgage financing requirements with the Federal Housing Administration (FHA). Many examples used in this book relate to the FHA mortgage financing program.

Down Payment of Funds "Before" Financing

Most mortgage lenders, especially the Federal Housing Administration (FHA), do not offer 100% financing of the home mortgage loans. Nonetheless, Veteran Administration (VA) will offer 100% financing of home mortgage loans. After purchasing a home, the buyer dwells in it and the property is now referred to as "owner occupied" ("o/o"). On the other hand, if a buyer does not occupy a home after purchasing, the property is known as a "non owner occupied" ("n/o/o"). The down payment for an owner occupied (o/o) property is about 3.5 % while the down payment for a non owner occupied (n/o/o) property is about 20%. When 3.5% of a loan is paid as down payment, the Loan-To-Value (LTV) of the property is (100% - 3.5%) 96.5%. If the down payment is 20%, the LTV is 80%. Prior to the economic meltdown in the USA, it was relatively easy to a find financial institution that would offer financial assistance to a buyer for property down payment.

Nowadays and due to the current economic recession in the country, the type of assistance is either very scarce or not available. In other words, if the purchase price of a home is $70,000, the down payment for o/o will be ($70,000 x 3.5%) $2,450 and the n/o/o will be ($70,000 x 20%) $14,000. The difference between these two payment scales is comparatively large. If the down payment is too high, the home buyer is encouraged to pursue a home in a lower price bracket, with a lower down payment amount. This plan is important because the mortgage lender will verify the down payment amount of the home owners before processing the loan. A more popular technique that people use for verifying finances is to have the buyers submit two or three consecutive months of their most recent bank statements. These statements will show credit balances of the owners for the two or three months. As a requirement, the bank balance needs to be enough to cover the down payment and closing cost of the presenting property. Otherwise, the processing of the loan will stop, pending an increase of funds in the bank balance.

The Closing Cost "Before" Financing

Closing cost varies, depending on the value of the property. Closing cost is calculated to cover Mortgage Insurance Payment (MIP), Hazard Insurance (HI), Real Estate Taxes, Broker's Fees, Title Fees, Appraisal Fees, Pre-Payments or Buy-Down Fees. A buy-down fee occurs when the borrower pays a lump sum of money to buy down or reduce applicable interest rate on the property. The size and sale price of a home frequently controls the payment in question. In the USA, closing cost in some states retains five per cent estimate of the acquired loan amount plus the MIP buy-down and down-payment costs. Some states control the closing cost by putting a limit on how much a closing cost can remain. Henceforth, it is the duty of the lenders to make sure that the closing cost stays within limits of the state laws. Other variables that may increase closing cost include, postponing the first mortgage payment date beyond the month following the closing date, the periodic interest amount, Mortgage Insurance Protection (MIP) fees and title insurance fees that go to protect a lender from any mistake the title company may make during the transaction activities. These figures or funds are generally added to the closing cost fees. Although, it is a requirement that home buyers buy title insurance for lenders, they may also wish to purchase insurance to protect against any mistake the title company makes on their home purchasing transactions. If a mistake occurs, the money will also be added to the closing cost. It may be worth mentioning that very often; many real estate buyers are not interested in buying the second title insurance. This is so because it results in the payment of extra fees to cover the same item - a mistake made by the Title Company. Since the title insurance companies do not have immunity from errors or fraud, some home buyers believe that it would be better, for the title companies to purchase their own "error and omission" insurance to protect them from their own mistakes. In fact, title companies have insurance that protects them. Nevertheless, they move to accept any coverage that an "uninformed" buyer is willing to pay. Moreover, many buyers wonder why it is legal for the home owners to pass on the payment of their Mortgage Insurance Protection (MIP) and Private Mortgage Insurance (PMI) to home lenders as approved by federal government. Actually, the cost for the triple protection of lenders (MIP/PMI, Hazard Insurance and Title Insurance), are passed down or paid by real estate buyers or home owners who are also borrowers.

Ratio Analysis "Before" Financing

Better prepared home buyers calculate all ratios, to prevent real estate underwriters from disqualifying their applications. A good debt ratio assures that a home buyer will have enough money to live on after making monthly mortgage payments. If the debt ratio is too high, a real estate buyer has the option of lowering it by either paying off the bill and eliminating one or two monthly debts on the loan application or opting to pay off some or all credit card loans and other incurred small charge accounts. The mortgage company may educate a buyer on how to accomplish this task. The facts in this "Reference Book" will help prepare a property buyer on what to expect from other entities that network in the purchasing and financing transactions. Real estate buyers do not need to memorize the contents of this book; instead, they should use it as a reference guide. It will be best to refer to this book when discussing a home or any other property purchase transactions.

The debt ratios often used in real estate financing are the front-end ratio and the back-end ratio. In some cases, the debt ratios are *28% - 45* % or below. However, some lenders accept a debt ratio of 50%. For Federal Housing Authority (FHA) loans, the front-end is *31%* while the back-end is *43%* (*31% / 43%*). On the contrary, the ratios for conventional loans are 28% / 36%.

Case Example

Frank wants to purchase a home that costs $72,000. His monthly income is $3,300 and he has other monthly bills amounting to $551. He uses the FHA option and his down payment of 3.5 per cent ($72,000 X 3.5 per cent) is $2,520. Therefore, the LTV amount of his loan ($72,000 – 2,520) is 69,480. Based on a thirty year loan financing with an Annual Percentage Rate (APR) of six percent, the monthly payment (with out escrow) amounts to about $450. A mortgage loan cost with "escrow" is one that includes the insurance and real estate tax figures of the subject (property). Frank's choice of FHA loan and FHA debt ratios are 31% for the front and 43% for the back. Frank's total monthly debt ratios can be estimated as follows.

Monthly Principal and Interest $(P + I)$ ---------------------- $ 450.00

Monthly Insurance payment --------------------------------- $50.00

Monthly Real Estate Taxes ------------------------------- $ 85.00

Other Monthly obligations, (Food and living expenses) $551.00

TOTAL MONTHLY DEBT ----------------------------- $ 1,136.00

Testing and Reconciling

Testing For the Front-End Ratio

The case example above shows that since Frank's monthly income is $3,300, his front-end qualifying figure will be: $3,300 x 31% = $1,023. This means that to qualify for the front-end loan requirement, Frank's monthly principal (p) and interest (I) monthly payment of (P + I) cannot exceed $1,023. Clearly, his P + I ($450), as shown above, are less than $1,023. Therefore, he is qualified for the front end ratio.

Testing For the Back-End Ratio

The monthly income of $3,300 x 43% = $1,419. The amount to be used for testing the back-end ratio must include P + I amount of the home, plus all other monthly expenses. This means that to qualify for the back-end ratio, Frank's total monthly payment of bills will not exceed $1,419. As we can see above, the total of Frank's P + I and all other monthly bills amount to $1,136, which is less than $1,419. Therefore, he qualifies for the back end ratio. Thus, the FHA debt ratios satisfy Frank's FHA mortgage loan.

Testing Debt Ratio for Non FHA Loan

With the income and loan amounts of Mr. Frank, it is possible to calculate his debt ratio for other types of loan program, such as the sub-prime loan. His total monthly debt is $1,136 and his total monthly income is $3,300. Therefore, his debt ratio ($1,136 divide by 3,300) is 35% which, is less than 50%. Evidently, his debt ratio is good.

Testing For the Closing Cost

In the USA, closing cost activities are unique in each state. Therefore, each state chooses and sets the amount. Closing cost limit in the State of Ohio is 5%. In fact, this 5% covers the commission for the Lender, Mortgage Broker, Title Company and other minor fees. Some activities that do not belong to this percentage include future interest figures for postponed payments, the mortgage insurance figure, the county deeds and other registration fees. The examples presented earlier in this text, are designed to assist a property buyer during purchasing and determine what techniques to use for a successful transaction outcomes. The lender or realtor may not figure out which way is best for the buyer. The buyer does this research for personal gains. A buyer, who has enough information, will be able to recognize when a lender or a realtor makes a mistake during a purchasing transaction.

Credit Endorsement "Before" Financing

Apart from the debt ratio, a lender uses other criteria to evaluate real estate loans. Usually, the approval or denial of a loan originates from the evaluation, opinion and confidence of the lender towards the borrower or the collateral offered by the borrower. A professional lender will generally, employ the principles of six Cs as a guide when assessing a borrower. It is important to note that some of the 6Cs may not affect or concern a home buyer directly but, may reveal some relevant facts. The 6Cs are listed and briefly described below.

1. Character helps to determine the degree of responsibility of a borrower.
2. Capacity helps to determine the size and volume of assets or income.
3. Capital helps to determine the cash flow and cash balance of a borrower.

4. Collateral helps to determine the worth and value of the mortgaged asset.
5. Condition helps to determine the economic trend of the applicant.
6. Communication helps to determine how much the applicant is able to comprehend.

Industrial deceitfulness causes "risky activities" and "frauds" during mortgage financing.

Character

A character or personality analysis helps to define a responsible home buyer or money borrower. In the end, this decision leads to risk reduction for the lender and buyer. Irresponsible home buyers will more likely than not, misuse their opportunities. For instance, some home owners mismanage their homes in multiple ways of including to engaging the illegal activities, invite neighbors, other citizens and law activities to evaluate these homes for potential abuse. If the homes are not properly maintained, the government repossesses them. Thereafter, lenders loose some or all of the money invested on the properties through loans. Very often, when such people are detected, their loan requests are denied, regardless of how promising their debt ratios are.

Capacity

Capacity judgment is a careful analysis of the magnitude in earning power of the home buyer. This is a reason why lenders demand two years income documents, check stubs and tax returns with W-2 forms from property purchasers. These documents help to determine the economic condition of growth concerning the borrower and his or her ability to make loan payments. For instance, if the personal income of a home buyer does not grow with personal needs of the buyer, it could mean that this buyer is not able to maintain the loan; hence the loan is more likely than not, to be denied.

Capital

Capital analysis consists of investigating cash flow and cash balance situations of the loan applicant. This analysis applies mostly to home buyers who are self-employed. The idea here is to look in the "Schedule C" (profit and loss statements). This document allows a person to see how dollars are made and how dollars are spent. Obviously, the mortgage lender will not favor the request of a mortgage applicant who has poor budgeting skills or does not show sufficient profit on his or her profit and loss statement (Schedule C). Therefore, profit shown on a schedule C will determine if the income of the borrower qualifies for the loan.

Collateral

Collateral is any mortgaged asset(s) acceptable to the lenders. The asset(s) presented as collateral must go through deep appraisal. This allows the lender to be certain that, in the case of a default, the value of the asset is enough to replace a delinquent account. A home owner may meet a collateral test because of a previously purchased home that can also serve as collateral for the mortgage loan. However, the appraisal of the property has to establish a value equal to or greater than the amount of the mortgage loan.

Condition

A complete ratio analysis helps to determine the condition of the borrower. Ratio analysis indicates the ability of the borrower to pay his or her maturing obligations. The calculations and explanations of the debt ratio analysis concerning a home or house buyer, is defined earlier in this text under "Ratio Analysis" category.

Communication

Good communication technique such as effective listening and body language will enhance development of the required ratio analysis in ways that benefit both parties (lender and borrower). Good communication strategies also boost future real estate engagements.

Industry Deceits

A home buyer ought to be aware of the most common fraud activities that exist in the real estate industry. These discrepancies happen very often and can happen to any buyer or borrower. The introduction of Acts by the government helps guide a person to utilize his/her legal rights while developing real estate financial contracts. These are explained in the next chapter.

CHAPTER FIVE
Mortgage Frauds And Cheating Methods

Real Estate Frauds

Real estate buyers need to be aware of industrial fraud and cheating methods before engaging in a real estate financing transactions. Research shows that there are mortgage frauds and/ or cheating activities in this industry. Indeed, mortgage frauds have contributed to significant financial losses to real estate buyers and financiers in the industry. In year 2004 Marta McCall, Senior Vice President of Risk Management Committee on Financial Services of United House of Representatives made a speech on "Fraud in Our Nation's Industry" she notes that fraudulent difficulties impair the real estate industry with a shadow. Mortgage fraud is the growing pervasive dark side of residential mortgage system that costs the industry and consumers millions and possibly billions, of dollars each year. She concludes by saying that today, mortgage industry leaders are extremely concerned that, this shadow has grown quite large in the past several years with the consequences devastating to lenders, taxpayers, consumers, communities and other cultures. Mortgage fraud comes in multiple dimensions. Examples include, flipping and skimming, which can be done by one person or a team of scam artists. Testifying in year 2000 in Washington, DC to the permanent subcommittee on investigation of fraud, Kenneth M. Donohue, says that the scheme is a typical flip because the investor contracts to purchase a property, recruit home buyers, partner with a crooked appraiser and engage a dishonest attorney to complete the resale and closing of the property at an inflated price. Finally, he states that, the illegality in property flipping arises because some team members in the real estate transactions conspire to inflate the value of a home. The same team members pocket the excessive profits at loan closings.

Equity skimming is a big concern in this real estate industry. A common form of equity skimming involves an investor who exploits a homeowner by taking an undue advantage of the home owner's lack of proper knowledge in the business. Property owners facing foreclosure or another financial stress need to be very vigilant and mindful of what they read and engage in before signing any document. Staying alert at all times, when making major transaction, helps to avoid or minimize fraudulent deals.

Definition of Real Estate Fraud

The research or survey phase of this book brought about multiple questions that potential buyers and sellers of properties would like to receive answers. These questions are rooted in mortgage frauds with emphases on predatory lending. These potential buyers and sellers communicate that they have some type of information about mortgage frauds. However, they would like to receive more knowledge in the area. Some of their questions are: what exactly is a mortgage fraud and what can a person do about it? What is predatory lending and what can anyone do about it? Why, when and, how are fraud activities able to work against a buyer? How many types of fraudulent activities are there? How can a buyer recognize a fraud.

Mortgage frauds are illegal offenses that can be divided in two parts. These frauds concern the acquiring or selling of property to make exaggerated profits. Studies agree that significant fraud practices are problematic in the real estate industry. It is generally known that the most common types of fraud involves falsifying financial qualifications, employments, income of loan applicants, securing inflated appraisals to increase loan amounts, stealing personal identities of applicants (identity fraud) and structuring real estate transactions with "straw buyers" who have no genuine interest in the properties however, would pose as prospective purchasers. A straw buyer is a person who is paid to allow the use of his name, credit scores, assets and other potent materials to purchase a house for another person. Straw buyers come with sufficient income and assets which of would qualify them to obtain mortgage loans on multiple owner occupied properties. In most cases, knowing and understanding types, of existing frauds, help to identify the executors.

Types of Real Estate Fraud

Certain persons answer the questions about the numbers and types of frauds that exist in the real estate industry. Usually, these frauds work to acquire real estate property to attain higher profits. Frauds are noted to be more rampant in the big cities than the small cities. This may be so because big cities are decorated with large real estate transactions. Further, longer cities receive and process higher volumes of loan requests than smaller cities. A higher volume of real estate transaction is more likely than not to lead more mistakes, dishonesties, misrepresentations and frauds, Prieston (2004).

Fraud for Real Estate Property

The first type is fraud for real estate property occurs when facts are purposely omitted, misrepresented or concealed for false acquisition of real estate property. The reason for committing a real estate of "fraud for property" depends on the executors. The activities can be further explained as follows:

- Fraud for property committed by a lender is mainly to falsely qualify for the purchase of a real estate property.
- Fraud for property, committed by a real estate seller is mainly to falsely sell or get rid of a property, faster than normal.
- Fraud for property, committed by a lender or a mortgage servicer is mainly for the purpose of taking over a real estate property in a deceitful manner. Often, omission of a critical potent clause nullifies the rights of a lender to repossess a property. The document may be misrepresented or forged and presented as authentic for approval, so that the court will take over the property, this type of fraud is usually rare.

Fraud for Higher Profit

Real estate sellers and lenders make profits because real estate practice is a profit making business. Fraud for higher profit occurs when real estate professionals work cooperatively (in groups or individually) to add unnecessary words, figures, misrepresent facts and distort or omit important facts on an important document, for the purpose of realizing more money that can lead to higher profits. Mostly, buyers do not involve themselves in fraud for profit. The real estate industry workforce, with potentials to involve in fraud activities leading to higher profits include: Financiers, Title Companies - also referred to as the Settlement

Companies, Surveyors, Insurance Companies, Appraisers, Mortgage Attorneys, Accountants, Underwriters, Mortgage Brokers and other company staff. Remember that the contents of this book are not intended to discredit or disconnect a person from acquiring the profit in a real estate transaction. Rather, it is written to create awareness to some of the practices that people engage in, within the real estate industry. Ultimately, everyone needs to remain vigilant in any business deal. Nevertheless, it is absolutely essential to remain vigilant while making any type of real estate transaction and avoid losing significant amount of money that create emotional pains. Examples of occurrences connecting real estate professionals are included in the appendices of this chapter.

Classifications of Real Estate Fraud

(i) Giving false information with case example.

(ii) Flipping.

(iii) Flagrant lies.

(iv) Lumping.

(v) Misleading.

(vi) Misrepresenting mortgage materials.

(vii) Predatory lending.

False Information

Case Example

Greg, a part-time worker making eight dollars per hour wants to purchase a home. Realizing that it is impossible for him to qualify for a mortgage loan, he conspires with his employer, who have prepared a report showing that he has a full-time employment and earns twenty-five dollars per hour. A lender approves a real estate mortgage loan for Greg, after verifying the report and Greg was able to purchase a home. The adverse effect in this fraud is that the buyer is not able to make the monthly mortgage payments since he does not have a gainful employment. After a few months, Greg (the buyer) loses the home and receives a foreclosure and repossession.

Flipping

Flipping fraud occurs when a property is sold and quickly re-sold in a few months. The main purpose of this activity is to increase the cost of the property for re-sale. The sellers involved in flipping properties, achieve higher profits. This type of fraud is usually directed to buyers and lenders. Flipping leads a lender to an unknowingly lend more money than is necessary towards the purchase of a home. The purchaser on the other hand, ends up with an unnecessary higher amount of mortgage loan. Moreover, if there is no potential buyer, the fraudulent seller may decide to use a straw buyer. A straw buyer is a property purchaser who has no interest in purchasing a property but, benefits in sharing profits with the seller.

Flagrant Lies and False Statements

A flagrant lie occurs when a buyer or seller intentionally gives false information on authentic documents. For instance, a seller deliberately inflates the price of a property and persuades a buyer to purchase the home quickly. The property purchaser may receive false information stating that the entire neighborhood will go through an upgrading process, which will significantly enhance the value of the property in the short run. Non vigilant buyers often fall victims of this type of scam. A deliberate lie insults and violates real estate laws, morals and ethics. A mortgage fraud for profit always touches the buyer and the lender in some ways.

Lumping

Lumping as mortgage fraud occurs when fictitious and unnecessary hidden figures and/or data are added (lumped) on an official document. The motive for lumping is mainly to realize larger amount of money as profits or commissions during the closing cost of a property Indeed, in some real estate closings, buyers pay little or no closing cost, but there are many other real estate closings where buyers pay thousands of dollars more than necessary. Some state legislations control closing cost by establishing a percentage limit to property closing cost. Studies show that in some states where the closing cost limit is five per cent, real estate purchasers can pay fees up to ten per cent. This action reveals fraud for higher income or profit. During foreclosure activities, fees and penalties that are derived from previous mortgage transactions are lumped together. Later, the lumping fee is added to the property closing cost and the property buyer pays all the fees.

Misleading

Misleading exists when a professional such as a seller on the transaction team, deliberately misdirects or deceives a purchaser away from the property of his/her choice. The purchaser is lead towards the property of seller's preference. For example, a realtor knowingly misdirects and directives a buyer to purchase a house that cost the same or lower, in an area the buyer does not fully appreciate. Real estate sellers who mislead buyers may do so for reasons, such as:

(a) The house being offered is not in the best condition.
(b) The home needs to be sold as soon as possible before it gets worse in deterioration.
(c) The house being offered to the purchaser is the only one available for sell.

Misleaders, usually, arrange and have home remodelers working in a dilapidated household at the time home purchasers visit to evaluate the property they may purchase. This professional, assures potential home buyers that the renovations and fixations of the home will be quick and ready to move-in before the purchasing transactions are completed. Once the closing deal is finalized and checks are issued, the misleading professional withdraws his home renovating staff and presents the unfinished home to the buyer - as ready. A few months after residing in the property, a purchaser notices that his new home is not ready. Subsequently, the misleading a professional avoids the attempts of the home buyer concerning the property. Misleading activities happen repeatedly in the real estate industry. Appendices 1 and 2 of this chapter show examples of misleading testimonies.

Misrepresentation

A misrepresentation shows that financial materials are concealed or purposely misinterpreted. This activity occurs when:

(a) Mortgage loan financing documents are intentionally omitted to hide relevant fact(s).
(b) Mortgage loan financing documents are wrongly interpreted to deliberately mislead people.

(c) Mortgage loan financing materials are deliberately distorted to create misunderstanding or miscommunication.

The real estate home buyer suffers damages resulting from misrepresentations in multiple ways that include purchasing or making proper mortgage loan decisions. Indeed, everyone participating in the real estate industry including the buyers commit this type of fraud. Types of documents that could easily be misrepresented are income documents, sales papers, sales contracts, purchasing data, closing cost figures and the monthly mortgage amounts that home purchasers pay. Misrepresentation type of fraud enhances higher advantages that meet the goal(s) or objective(s) of the person pushing the fraud.

Predatory Lending

Predatory lending is unacceptable, unethical and fraudulent. Mortgage fraud does not include predatory lending per se, but rather relates more specifically to the types of fraud perpetrated, on lenders and borrowers, Prieston (2004). Notably, predatory lending is mostly committed by some professionals in the real estate industry who network to execute the fraud. Predatory lending occurs frequently during money lending transactions. Many lenders participate in this type of fraud, because their work specifications have loop holes that allow them to benefit significantly from the industry. They deceive real estate purchasers and falsely obtain potent information from them to increase profits. In the short-run, the target of this fraud manipulates and misrepresents mortgage interest rates in ways that yield more money. In the long-run, the fraud replicates periodic changes in monthly mortgage payment figures that yield more money for personal gains. Predatory lending is practiced in many ways. Lenders using this tactics often target the most vulnerable population including elderly, women, persons with disabilities and people in the low income bracket, Welcher (2010). Predatory loans harm borrowers by making payment maintenance very difficult or impossible. Note that if mortgage payments are missed, the purchaser of the property risks losing the property. This is one reason why it seems difficult for a person making real a estate deal, to engage in a fixed monthly mortgage payment that remains fixed during its entire life. Predatory lending yields confusing and higher cost loans for property purchasers. Lenders, who engage in the practices, make misleading deals to purchase that often the result in home foreclosures, home repossessions, home abandonments and poverty for the victims. Ultimately, a lesson to learn from predatory lending is that profit making, in business transactions, need to represent a win-win situation, for both buyers and sellers.

Sometimes, buyers become victims of fraud due to ignorance of rules and regulations. However, reading and understanding this "reference" book may protect potential victims in many ways. A property buyer working alone, may not be mentally, emotionally or spiritually prepared. This person has a higher risk of falling prey to predators. Predators take undue advantage of the vulnerabilities of such a buyer. When a purchaser approaches a lender for a mortgage loan transaction, the lender educates the purchaser with very few mortgage information such as Fixed Mortgages (FM), Variable Rate Mortgage (VRM) or Adjustable Rate Mortgage (ARM). These represent a fraction of the mortgage products a buyer can select from. The VRM or ARM has interest rates that adjust periodically, as stated in the mortgage contract.

The interest rates adjust monthly or yearly, depending on the terms of the contract. It is important to note that in this type of situation, the terms of the contract, depends on the property a buyer chooses to mortgage. Sometimes, lenders may invite or lure buyers to choose the ARM mortgages due to higher profits they yield to lenders. A sub-prime mortgage is very attractive when a lender shows that the fixed mortgage has an interest rate of six per cent while the interest rate for the ARM is only 3/2%. The 3/2% explains that interest rate for the first 2 years is 3% and thereafter it adjusts (usually higher) in accordance to the index rate economy of the country. Thus, a home buyer with an ARM deal could be making monthly payments of $400 for the first two years, $600 the third year and $900 the fourth year and so forth. The same rate will increase every year until the rate cap is reached. The margin used to calculate increase in payments must be specified in the mortgage agreement. When the interest rate increases, the monthly payment will go up and the home owner may default on the loan. Loan defaults always lead to foreclosure with repossession. In fact, millions of foreclosures with or without repossessions result from ARM or VRM mortgage loans. This lending technique is daunting demoralizing to the victims and the real estate industry. The practice increases profit margins and creates direct adverse affects on the buyers.

Fraud Activities by Other Entities

Federal Housing Administration (FHA) - Fraud Activities

Fraudulent activities can exist in all types of real estate transactions, including the FHA (government insured) loans. In the past, FHA lenders have been criticized for being less strict with some real estate lending professionals and working inefficiently with federal government insured loans. Indeed, foreclosing FHA loan results in the federal government refunding and outstanding funds to the mortgage lender. While verifying the testimony of Czerwinski in 1999 to a subcommittee on investigations concerning FHA performances, Senator Collins reports that some lenders with questionable proficiencies are approved to work in the real estate financial industry. Further, he notes that even lenders, who clearly have rating problems with about 40 percent of the mortgages they process and receive approvals. Further, he says that it is notable that although lenders receive refunds, buyers make monthly payments for the FHA insurance which insures lenders. If this is so, lenders may help purchasers by lowering the interest rates for each mortgage loan to 2% or less because they enjoy complete protection at the expense of the buyers.

Title Companies or Settlement Agents – Fraud Activities.

Title companies are also known as the settlement agents because the USA law requires that they perform all mortgage loan closings. This law makes it illegal for a mortgage company, realtor, lender or any other real estate entity to close a real estate mortgage deal. Although, title companies do not participate in loan processing, nevertheless, they are able to recognize a fraudulent document. The question now is, what type of actions do title companies take when they detect fraudulent activities? Since there is no perfection in human behaviors, how then does anyone discover when a title company is gainfully participating with a fraud team? The awareness of this type of fraud comes as a result contemporary knowledge in making good transactions. In any case, a title agent with questionable character can execute a serious mortgage fraud. In any case, buyers and lenders need to be alert and watch out for illegal transactions.

The Appraisers - Fraud Activities

A professional appraiser is a person who is licensed or certified by the state, to visit and provide authentic assessments of a house or property listed for sale. A professional appraiser takes pictures of the interior, exterior, measures the yards, determines monetary value and writes a relative report about the house. The work of a professional appraiser is called an "appraisal" of the property. This report, guides a lender to properly assess the worth of a house. Like other insiders (staff) in the real estate industry, an appraiser can present false documentations. A false document, whether prepared in good faith or not, will result in the increase or decrease in value of a real estate mortgage loan. For instance, if an appraiser falsely represents the value of a home as two hundred thousand dollars when, the home is worth eighty thousand dollars, the mortgage lender will be deceived to lend about two hundred thousand dollars for the purchase of a house that is less in value. In other words, a fraudulent appraisal increases or decreases the Loan to Value (LTV) of a mortgage loan.

This narrative shows that a certified appraiser appraised five homes in the name of a woman. Evidently, the income of this woman, although in the low income bracket, is used to purchase all five homes that is worth resulting five hundred thousand ($500,000) dollars. A title company has recruited an appraiser that appraised the properties. The first contractors, on the team, made payment to the appraiser in advance, while the second contractor provided driving license and two years tax returns belonging to the aunt of the second contractor. This aunt has a stable job and an excellent credit reports. Next, the appraiser presents five appraisal reports for the five different homes and moved out of state leaving no forwarding information.

Authentic documents concerning the homes were submitted to the bank or financial institution that approved five different mortgage loans. These loans amounted to about $580,000. Subsequently, the contractor engaged his female friend who impersonates his aunt and signed the checks. The money realized from this crooked deal would then be shared by each participant on the fraud team. The victim of these happenings had no knowledge of the activities until monthly bills for five different homes arrived at her residence. A second problem arose when the victim discovered that none of the homes were valuable. Finally, unable to find solution to these problems from someone or a government agency, she filed bankruptcy. Additionally, she endured the hardship of personal bad credit reports that could trouble her for Noteworthy is the fact that the victim of fraud in this case had no interest in purchasing a home.

An independent business man, whose business is overdrawn, teams up with an appraiser, a Title Company and other individuals who are willing to distort figures and present them as accurate data. Some of these players are straw buyers, willing to buy homes that do not exist. It is noted that this team has been engaging in fraudulent operations for many years and have embezzled eight million dollars, from the real estate industry. In the end, he is sentenced to serve time in prison.

Completing a successful real estate deal requires the work of efficient Appraisal Agency and Title Company. Sometimes, depending on the State where a deed occurred, it is not easy to file a legal action against an appraiser and win. While Appraisers can be liable for their negligence, a successful action against a careless appraiser is dependent on:

(1) The state laws in which the action is brought.
(2) The type of action brought against the appraiser i.e. negligence or misrepresentation.
(3) Whether the lender bringing the action retained the appraiser.

The same fraudulent situation can occur with FHA loan transactions, if the FHA is not efficient. The GOA has found that FHA (HUD) is not doing a good job monitoring the work of appraisers and holding them accountable for the quality of their work where the problem of property flipping is concerned, Czerwinsiki (2000). Examples of authentic appraisal documents are included in the appendix of this chapter.

Adverse Effects of Mortgage Fraud

(a) Lenders lose thousands, millions or billions of dollars and/ or time annually.
(b) Buyers lose thousands, millions or billions of dollars and/ or time annually.
(c) Real Estate industry loses an undetermined amount of money and prestige annually.

(d) General public (Taxpayers) lose millions or billions of dollars annually. Taxpayers were billed out of more than $35 million in a single scam, (Marta McCall, 2004).

(e) Community and multiple neighborhoods - lose money, prestige, appearance and home appreciation annually. Loosing home appreciation value is critical because it is what serves as the future return on investment (ROI) for most home owners.

Legal Rights of Home Purchasers

Sometimes, it is easy to mislead a buyer or a seller when making real estate transactions; especially, if the type of misrepresentation activity is new to the industry. However, buyers or sellers in a lot of cases, fall victims because they are not aware of their legal rights. This reference book is programed to help buyers know and understand their basic legal rights and what to do about them. The Federal Government has passed multiple rules and regulations that award some mortgage loan rights to purchasers. A home purchaser or seller, who does not understand necessary legal implications, remains at risk for a deceitful transaction. The legal rights include the following.

Caveat Emptor (CE)

Caveat emptor notes that too much of anything is bad. In other words, if a real estate deal sounds too good to be true, chances are that it is not a good deal.. A person making a real estate transaction, needs to utilize the skills of professional consultants to achieve better end results

Fair Credit Reporting Act (FCRA)

The FCRA or Regulation V is a federal law passed in 1970. FCRA authorizes buyers to access their credit information as needed, in the process of acquiring mortgage loans. Apart from emphasizing the rights of the home purchasers, this Act establishes guidelines for responsibilities to the lenders (creditors) and the credit bureau systems. The law ensures that the responsibilities are fair, accurate and protect the personal information of borrowers.

Fair and Accurate Credit Transaction Act (FACTA)

The 2003 FACTA reinforces or amends the FCRA. Unfortunately, identity theft crime was introduced after the passage of the FCRA. The FACTA helps the buyers (borrowers), fight the crime of identity theft, especially when the credit information of a borrower is abused or tampered. If this happens, the borrower can freeze the credit information or declare a fraud alert. A fraud alert requires the credit bureau to check with the borrower before releasing his or her credit data to anyone or entity who requests the information.

Equal Credit Opportunity Act (ECOA)

This Act of 1974 or Regulation B is very favorable to buyers because it plays a significant role in eliminating discriminatory practices against buyers, especially minorities, such as females and other citizens who are frail. It is alleged that women do not receive as their male counterpart when applying for mortgage loans. Further, ECOA authorizes that the income from public assistance programs be recognized and approved for credit purposes. These incomes include from pension, annuity, retirement, child support and alimony. Further, a buyer who receives public assistance can incorporate it as part of his/her income to qualify for a mortgage loan. After the passage of the ECOA, financial institutions began to disregard race, religion, color, national origin, gender, age and marital status of a person in granting loan approvals. However, it is allowed to ask buyers certain questions to help in gathering demographic data for special purposes.

Home Mortgage Disclosure Act (HMDA)

Although this Act of 1975 or Regulation C applies directly to control the financiers, it also helps buyers or credit applicants in many other ways. For instance, HMDA monitors the discrimination and lending practices which have been outlawed by the ECOA. Examples are how loan officers treating the concept of race, gender and ethnic groups. By monitoring the lending habits of financiers, HMDA is able to discover when "Red Lining" is practiced in any credit transaction. Red Lining exists when a loan applicant is refused a loan because he/she is buying a home in an area where people of his/her color or ethnic group are not wanted.

Truth in Lending Act (TILA)

TILA is a federal law passed in 1968 as title one of the "Consumer Credit Protection Act" (CCPA). Its main objective is to protect the consumers or buyers. The terms of this law are as follows:

(a) Financiers need to disclose the cost and terms of credits to borrowers.
(b) Financiers should disclose a TILA form that highlights the annual percentage rate, finance charge; amount financed and total payments. This type of action helps a property

buyer to review loan figures and decide on acceptance or rejection of the loan.

(c) Financiers should establish identical standards and methods for exhibiting credits and loan costs.

(d) Financiers should encourage borrowers or buyers to shop around before making a decision to accept a loan offer. Financiers should explain to buyers that having signed papers (apart from the closing papers), does not mean that they must eventually accept the loan.

(e) Financiers should make sure that a buyer who has an ARM loan, also has a "CHARM Booklet" to properly inform him or her of the risks associated with the loan.

(f) Financiers should advise buyers to retain and read all disclosures and booklets given to them.

(g) Financiers should give each borrower a completed Truth In lending (TIL) loan form within three business days from the date the complete application is received and at the loan closing.

(h) Financiers must give and re-disclose to a borrower the TIL and Good Faith Estimate (GFE) cost forms, seven days before the closing date.

(i) Financiers must re-disclose and give the same forms to a borrower whenever the Annual Percentage Rate (APR) of the loan changes by more than .125 (1/8) %.

(j) Financiers should inform borrowers or buyers, at loan closing, their rights to rescind faulty loans and the rescinding can be executed any day, including Saturdays except Sundays and Federal public holidays.

(k) Financiers must always use truthful and substantiating words in their advertising.

This Act, also called Regulation Z, can be used to combat foreclosure in multiple ways. The APR must be disclosed.

Real Estate Settlement Protection Act (RESPA)

The RESPA of 1974 is said to be the biggest protection Act for real estate buyers. Like TILA, it changes and modifies other acts. Real estate property buyers need to take note of the different provisions of this Act. The purpose of this Act is to protect buyers, such as:

(a) Protect from excessive settlement costs.

(b) Protect from improperly earned or charged fees.

(c) Assist buyers to obtain the closing documents with closing cost, earlier than the closing date so that they can have time to shop around for lowest cost.

The Real Estate Settlement Protection Act (RESPA)
Requirements
Good Faith Estimate (GFE)

GFE is a statement implying good faith measures that a loan originator develops and a borrower or a buyer signs. This testimony is called good faith estimate because the form contains the estimated figures of the closing cost and the law requires that the estimate be in prepared in good faith. The obligations of GFE are as follows:

(a) The lender must deliver a signed copy of the GFE to the borrower within three business days after receiving the completed application, but it does not have to be given until the buyer selects a property to purchase.

(b) The form must be re-disclosed and re-given in conjunction with the TIL form seven days before the loan closing.

(c) The prepared GFE form should include:

    (i) The term of the loan.

    (ii) The interest percentage of the loan.

    (iii) The closing cost of the loan.

    (iv) The balloon payment of the loan.

    (v) The pre-payment cost of the loan.

(d) Charges the GFE borrower receives include the following.

    (i) The origination charges.

    (ii) The charges for locking the interest rates.

    (iii) Other adjusted charges and costs.

(e) Adjusted Charges Exceeding Limits: If the following costs are adjusted to exceed those on the original GFE by more than 10 %, the buyer has the right to reject the loan or the excess costs. Rules and regulations that guide the treatment of excess cost are:

    (i) Settlement charges (closing costs), if the lender has chosen the title company.

    (ii) Any lender required services, such as the title services, title insurance, and so forth, if the lender has chosen them.

    (iii) All government recorded charges.

    (iv) Any excess by more than 10 % must be refunded to the buyer within 30 days after the loan closing.

(f) Revised Charges: If a GFE document is revised, the new form must contain the reasons for changing the figures included in the original GFE. Also the original and revised GFE must be kept for three years.

Three RESPA Sections Favorable to the Rights of Home Buyers
Section 6 - Rights of Buyers Regarding Loan Service Transfer

These rights are listed below:

(i) Buyers will receive servicing disclosure three business days after the application.

(ii) Buyers must receive adequate notices whenever a loan is sold or transferred.

(iii) Buyer must receive a service transfer notice 15 days prior to the transfer.

(iv) Buyer will receive a sale transfer notice 15 days prior to the sale.

(v) Buyer must receive 15 days notice from the new owner after the transfer.

(vi) Buyer will receive 15 days notice from the new owner after the sale.

(vii) Buyer should not be charged a late fee before 60 days during the transfer period.

Section 8 - Rights of Buyers to Reject
Illegal Business Practices
Buyers have the right to reject:

(i) Exchange of valuable items, including money among the insider professionals.

(ii) Adding unnecessary, unreasonable and unearned fees to the costs of the buyers.

(iii) Kickbacks of money or goods or both between the professionals.

(iv) Sham business which is an illegal joint venture to split the money of the buyer.

(v) Therefore, buyers have the right to receive an affiliated business disclosure to discover when illegal acts are practiced in the process preparing the loan.

Section 10 - Rights of Buyers Regarding the Escrow Accounts:
These rights include:

(i) Lenders must provide buyers with the "Initial Escrow Statement" for the first year of

(ii) the loan, at the closing or within 45 days thereafter.

(iii) Lenders must provide to buyers an annual "Escrow Account Analysis".

(iv) Lenders maintain Escrow Cushion Limit of about one sixth of yearly disbursement.

(v) An Escrow Balance exceeding $50, should be returned to the borrower within 30 days.

Hud-1 Settlement Statement

This is a very important closing statement which shows expenses to be paid by the buyer and the seller. The document also, shows the amount borrowed and closing cost which the buyer has to pay. The lender or the title company must give a copy of this statement to the buyer twenty-four hours before the closing. This will allow the buyer to review all debit and credit statements, decide what figures to reject or accept and decide whether or not to proceed with the closing deal. If accepted, RESPA mandates that the closing can take place at the office of the lender, the office of the title company or the place of the buyer.

Other RESPA Rights Given to Buyers

A buyer has to receive the "Settlement Cost Booklet" called "Buying Your Home" within three days following a home purchase. The book educates the new home owner on loan servicing, inherent risks and the right to complain.

The owner of an open-ended loan, such as the home equity loan, shall receive a booklet called "When Your Home Is on the Line." Again, this booklet educates the buyer on all relevant information. This Act is called Regulation X. Hopefully, the data and other information exposed in this text will help buyers and sellers make better real estate deals. Indeed, the readers of this book will acquire enough knowledge that will enable them to discuss, negotiate and consummate deals successfully in the real estate industry. There are many other government acts; however, those commented on are mostly advantageous to borrowers, buyers, sellers and builders in the real estate industry.

CHAPTER SIX
Plans And Actions "During" Mortgage Financing

Classifications of Funding or Financing Sources

Multiple sources of funds are enumerated and classified later in this chapter. Home buyers must select those that meet their funding needs. Generally, people sell houses for profit. In fact, many mortgage lenders will not consider a mortgage loan under $50,000. In a situation of a poor economy (such as recession) many people are able to purchase homes for smaller amounts, which may range from under $10,000 to over $50,000. These potential buyers need to know and understand the sources of funds available in their localities. Some sources of funds will lend any amount of money while others limit themselves to lending smaller or larger amounts of money to borrowers. It is good to note that due to fluctuation in fund supplies, interest rates tend to vary among financial sources. For instance, the loans from Finance Companies may cost more than the loans from other Mortgage Bankers mainly as a result of higher interest rates.

This section explains short-term and long-term financing. Short-term financing mostly concerns smaller amounts of funds that come with higher interest rate while the long-term financing usually concern larger amounts of funds with lower interest rates. Financing is usually divided into levels of first, second and third sources. The loan applicants find it easier to quality for the first level of financing sources. Most times, a first level lender runs the risk of losing the loan funds due to lack of sufficient collateral(s) from applicants. This is a fundamental reason why first level financing sources have higher interest rates than the second of third level of financing sources.

First Level Funding Sources Include, (Igah, 1983)

1. IOU ("I owe you" person to person transaction, no lending license required).
2. Bank credit cards.
3. Business loans from a friendly company.
4. Installment certificates.
5. Collateral trust bonds.
6. Participation mortgage certificate.
7. Cooperatives.
8. Individual licensed money lenders.
9. Banks - personal loans.
10. Finance companies.
11. Credit unions.
12. Loan agents.
13. Sellers.
14. Life insurance policy loans.
15. Savings and loans agencies.
16. Second mortgage companies - personal property.
17. Pawn agents.

Second Level

It is more difficult to qualify for the second level funding sources than the first level because of the requirements. The lenders using the second level of financial sources are firmer with business protocols than those with first level financing sources. Also, the loans from a second level involve more money than loans from the first level.

Second Level Funding Sources Include

1. Second mortgage companies - personal and non-personal property.
2. State bank loans.
3. Land contracts.
4. Builders.
5. Revolving line of credit.
6. Commercial paper.
7. Pledged savings account loan.
8. Collateral trust bonds.
9. Real estate agents.
10. Trustees of estates.
11. Real estate syndicates.
12. Line of credits.

Third Level Funding Sources Include

This is the most difficult level for loan applicants to qualify. This level usually requires one hundred per cent collateral, full appraisal and underwriting. In most cases, the money to be borrowed belongs to the public or stockholders funds. This level of funding includes:

1. First mortgage companies or bankers.
2. National banks.
3. Mortgage brokers.
4. Commercial banks.

5. Saving and loans institutions.
6. Real estate investment trusts.
7. Life insurance companies.
8. USA government.
9. Foundations.
10. Real estate bonds issuance.
11. Real estate stocks issuance.
12. Long term lease.

Noteworthy is the fact that home mortgage financing is a third level engagement. It is necessary to know that the levels of financing are not rigid. For instance, the entities on higher levels can provide funds to any lower level entity. In other words, level three can provide loans or funds for levels one or two. Likewise, level two may provide funds for level one. Moreover, a lending institution may be able to supply the first, second or third level financing for a particular type of investment. Thus, any of the above classification is not rigid. (Igah, 1983).

Real Estate Negotiation

When the ratios and funds of a buyer meet the loan requirements, the next step is to select the subject property. In the real estate industry, the home or house that a buyer wishes to purchase with a mortgage loan is the "subject property." At this stage of making plans and implementing actions during financing, it is imperative that home buyers remain vigilant with negotiation skills in critical areas such as price, date, time, condition, location of property and possible monetary additions from the real estate seller. A reasonable purchase price depends on the negotiation skills of the buyer. Advantages of good negotiation techniques are discussed later in this text.

To arrive at a good negotiation price, a buyer or a seller must first determine a reasonable goal before engaging in negotiations. Usually, the amenities in a property will play a role in determining the price range and monthly mortgage payments on the property. The buyer may have a limit on an acceptable and affordable monthly mortgage payment. Likewise, the seller may establish a comfortable ceiling price. The negotiation skills of a person go a long way to determine if the specified goal will be achieved. Hence, a goal governs or controls the offer and acceptance of a person. Good negotiators always focus on their needs and at the same time attempt to understand the goal of the other negotiator(s). Finally, good negotiators understand what their interests represent and they can formulate the offer they present to satisfy both their interests and those of the other party. Generally, negotiators do not disclose their bottom line offer to their competitors. Also, good negotiators hide emotional feelings during a negotiation exercise. Anyone who attends a hearing in a court case will learn that a good judge does not reveal feelings that will lead anyone to make conclusive judgments on a case.

Types of Mortgage Products

Mortgage loans are third preference level as previously explained. The most difficult financing level for loan applicant to achieve is the third preference level. This means that a home buyer must pay special attention to detail making sure that the mortgage is adequate and meets specified needs. Good appraisers work to assist mortgagors in achieving their goals. Before choosing a mortgage product, a home buyer selects an option from the different types of mortgage products listed later in this chapter. If more details are needed, the home buyer must research on the subject or consult a real estate expert. At this stage, a buyer would have selected a home, qualified for the front and back end ratios, reserved money for the down payment and saved enough money for the closing cost. Next are examples of types of mortgage products.

Federal Housing Administration (FHA) - Insured Mortgage

In 1934, the USA's congress passed the National Housing Act (NHA), which created the Federal Housing Administration (FHA). The FHA encourages construction and ownership of new homes. All FHA mortgages are insured by the Federal Housing Administration. Under this act, a mortgagor can borrow up to 97% of the value of the home being purchased and the remaining 3% are provided as down payment. Although the FHA loan will finance one to four family dwellings, it sometimes finances construction jobs, including home improvements, repairs and alterations on existing structures. It is helpful to note that the FHA is not a mortgage lender and the fundamental obligation of the FHA is to insure mortgage debts against losses. If the mortgagor whose loan is insured by the FHA fails to make needed payments, FHA will refund the mortgagee up to 97 % of the loss, after subtracting the amount of money used as the down payments. To protect against this insurance loss, the mortgagor pays a monthly percentage of insurance premium charges, on the loan balance. Finally, both the lender and the borrower must meet the necessary qualifications to benefit from the FHA loan.

Veteran Administration (VA) - Guaranteed Mortgage

The VA mortgage features the Readjustment Act of 1944 for the USA service men, as amended and the GI Bill (Korea) of July 1952. Precisely, a VA mortgage loan is guaranteed by the Veteran Administration. The VA loan offers some protection to a mortgage depending on the loan qualification. Examples of such coverage are the principal amount, interest, taxes, repairs and insurance. Although, the VA loan requires an insurance premium payment, it pays foreclosure cost for the mortgagor. Both mortgagor and mortgagee must meet the necessary qualifications to benefit from the VA mortgage services.

The Conventional Mortgage

A mortgage loan that is not insured by FHA and not guaranteed by the VA is a conventional mortgage loan. A conventional loan usually requires higher amount of mortgage down payments. However, there may be an occasion when the employer of a home buyer or any other reputable finance entity guarantees or insures the mortgage loan of a property buyer. A properly insured mortgage loan is also classified as conventional if it is not FHA or VA guarantee insurance.

The Package Mortgage

A Package Mortgage is a transaction that enables a borrower to consolidate and procure all loans from one source. A package is when a real estate contains chattels, such as different types of appliances including range, refrigerator and dishwasher. Therefore, the deal becomes a package deal and the loan like it, is a package loan. Another advantage of a Package Mortgage is that the interest rate on the appliances is much less than the prevailing rate, especially if the chattels are set up for monthly installment payments.

The Blanket Mortgage

This is a loan that covers properties including two or more homes or lots. Some people own or have multiple homes (up to forty homes or even more) and may also own other real properties. People who own lots of real properties may benefit more from financing or re-financing all the properties through one lender and acquire a blanket mortgage. Usually, this type of mortgage contains a partial release clause which details the release price of properties individually. This makes it possible for the mortgagor to sell a home or a lot, if necessary. A partial release clause must be included to prevent a buyer from risking foreclosure on all the properties if the blanket loan is defaulted and/or foreclosed.

The Budget Mortgage

A budget mortgage is generally referred to as a PITI mortgage which means Principal, Interest, Taxes and Insurance. The PITI is set to meet all payment aspects of the mortgage. Part of the mortgage paid must go to satisfy the principal, interest, real estate taxes and insurance. Essentially, the borrower pays one-twelfth of the yearly amount every month. Sometimes it is referred to as an "escrow" account. In the past years, a borrower was able to make decisions with the option to accept or refuse an escrow account arrangement. If a property buyer accepts this concept, the mortgagee will collect monthly property taxes and insurance from the owner and make payments to the appropriate creditors. Also, If a property buyer refuses this model, the property owner will make the necessary payments for the insurance and real estate taxes. Currently, many lenders, especially FHA, prefer to make it mandatory for a borrower to accept an escrow account arrangement.

The Open-End Mortgage

The open-end mortgage is similar to the second mortgage. Under this condition, a buyer may finance two-thirds of a real property with a lender. However, this technique allows a buyer or a borrower to choose to finance the remaining one-third value of the loan with a different lender, if a need arises. This arrangement can be effective without violating the terms of the first mortgage. Subsequently, the second lender takes a second mortgage on the property. Choosing a second lender is a good option if the total mortgage does not exceed the full value of the property.

The Close-End Mortgage

The close-end mortgage is the opposite of the open-end type. In this situation, the borrower is not allowed to acquire any additional loan amount on the property. The essential function of the close-end mortgage agreement is to protect the interest of the mortgage lender. Each home buyer needs to make sure that this clause is not included in the mortgage agreement of the home purchase. In fact, the contents of this book are not enough to demonstrate all the related findings. Thus, proper research or consultation with a real estate professional team or an agent will help to bring about better efficacy to the mortgage arrangement process. Having a close-end plan makes it more difficult for the home owner to obtain a second mortgage, in the future. After maintaining consistency with making mortgage payments for some years, a home owner accumulates equity on the home. At this time, the home owner may cash out money he or she needs, through re-financing the property. The funds cashed out may be used for future home investments. The home buyer can also take a second mortgage on the property and use the proceeds to stabilize other potent goal.

The Participation Mortgage

The participation mortgage is one that has more than one mortgagee. Generally, the amount of money borrowed with the participation mortgage method is so large that it becomes necessary for several creditors to participate in the operation. In the end, the creditors distribute the rewards among themselves. The mortgage agreement will state how much each creditor seeks from the principal, how many shares from the return each receives, and the meeting site to engage in proper discussions. Engaging in a participation mortgage is a very beneficial concept in a financially tight or depressed economy.

The Purchase Money Mortgage

The Purchase Money Mortgage (PMM) is popularly known as "PM Mortgage." The PM Mortgage is specified on the mortgage document because every home buyer is required to recognize it. In PM Mortgage deals, the seller does the financing. For instance, if the sale price of a home is $50,000 and the buyer has $20,000, the seller accepts the $20,000 and takes a mortgage agreement on the remaining $30,000. In other words, the buyer makes a down payment and the seller, not a bank, takes a mortgage on the property for the remaining $30.000. Usually, the seller gives a reasonable interest rate for the mortgage deal.

Construction or Building Mortgage Loan

Construction loan is designed to assist a builder acquire necessary funds for erecting new buildings or reconstructing existing ones. A real estate participant needs to be aware of the fact that construction or building mortgage loan does not necessarily concern home buyers directly. After building a home, the costs of the production are passed on to a property purchaser. Generally, the borrower does not receive the full amount of the loan at the time of home closing.

The terms of the building or mortgage contract will specify intervals at which a borrower will receive financial disbursements. Final disbursement of funds is made with the contractor after completing the building project. Next, the lender or the agent performs a comprehensive inspection to confirm that the property is in compliance with the agreed construction plans and with all government requirements. Both lender and borrower benefit greatly from a construction mortgage loan. The borrower may not worry about interest payments until the financial disbursements become productive and the property is available to him or her. On the other hand, a lender does not disburse any part of the loan until it is certain that the property in construction is making satisfactory progress. However, in some states, lenders demand interest payments from the first day of loan payment. The argument here is that the money for construction is already set aside for the borrower to use, exclusively, for construction purposes. It is best to understand that the state laws before making any type of real estate transactions

The Junior Mortgage

A junior mortgage, as described earlier, is usually a subordinate loan as a second mortgage. This means that if the mortgagor defaults, the lien of the senior lender will be paid in full before considering the obligation of the junior mortgage lender. This situation is similar to taking a second mortgage on a property. A foreclosure may not be unfavorable to the junior mortgage lender due to inability to realize enough funds from selling the property. However, the junior mortgage lender can try to remedy the situation or, at least, mitigate losses by buying the property from the senior mortgage lender at the balance of the loan payments. This purchaser may proceed to make necessary improvements on the property and advance to resale the property gainfully. Under this condition, the junior mortgage lender stands to make some profits due to the appreciation value of the property.

Trust Deed Mortgage

Many states make use of trust deed mortgages. This is when an authentic instrument is prepared and used to convey a trust to a third person holding the property. The holder becomes the trustee who the lender trusts. The trustee has the obligation to implement the contract requirements accurately, legally and ethically in order to help dismiss or mitigate defaults. By doing so, the entire contracting process will be faster and easier to consummate.

Strong Mortgage Instruments

Two other types of loans that hold strong and genuine mortgage instruments are Land and Balloon Contracts. These contracts are more ways to assist a purchaser in financing homes/

houses. Any of these contracts can be rewarding. On the whole, Land Contract and Balloon Contract are riskier than other contracts.

Land Contract Mortgage

A land contract is the practice that allows a buyer to engage in a property deal with little or no down payments. The potential buyer negotiates to buy a property and make monthly payments as agreed upon. The seller (owner) retains the title and ownership of the property until the completion of all payments. Land Contract method can also be used for other purchases that are not real estate properties such as automobiles, furniture and appliances. This practice is usually a first mortgage financing and does not necessarily belong to the third level funding sources even though it links closer to the first level sources. Sometimes, the I Owe You (IOU) which is occasionally referred to as person to person funding source, portrays the awareness that sellers are willing to extend land contracts to buyers. As a precaution, a buyer needs to understand the contract before signing any documents. The buyer loses the deal if any portion of the contract is missing such as violating the two consecutive mortgage payments agreement. The seller (owner) does not have to undergo the necessary legal foreclosing procedure to take over the property. He simply disregards the Land Contract agreement, as if it never existed. The seller may also take over or resell the property to a new buyer. Moreover, the seller retains all previously made mortgage payments as rent payments. In other words, if a default occurs, the prospective home buyer looses everything in the deal. This is a fundamental reason why a Land Contract mortgage instrument is classified as a "strong" category.

Balloon Mortgage Contract

A balloon contract is a purchase contract that requires the last payment of the debtor to be much larger than the preceding payments made. This technique is mostly used by owner-sellers of real estate to provide financing to their buyers, who cannot readily qualify to obtain standard mortgage loans. This is a first mortgage financing category that mostly belongs to the first level sources of fund as previously discussed. It is usually an arrangement between sellers and buyers. Balloon mortgage contract also allows a purchaser more time to rectify credit issues and qualify for a typical mortgage financing; that allows a home purchaser to obtain mortgage loan from a banker or a financial institution when needed. The buyer who is willing to sign a balloon contract needs to make sure that his/her credit issues can be fixed in about two years or as contracted. Another reason for accepting this type of loan is to have more freedom to pay-off some personal credit report debts, obtain and present receipts to the credit bureaus and raise the credit scores within the next two years. If this is consummated properly, the results will make it possible to obtain standard financing while the balloon contract is in effect. While concentrating on the improvement of credit scores, a person should also keep an eye on the financial ratios as well as other mortgage financing requirements that may vary. The consequence of violating a balloon contract is similar to that of a land contract where the buyer takes a loss in the investment previously made.

Noxious Real Estate Purchase Mistake

In this situation, a home buyer needs to maintain serious alertness when selecting a property to buy. Any error made in the process of purchasing a real estate property can be very expensive. This is partly because unlike smaller purchases, it is almost impossible to exchange or return a real estate property after financing. For instance, let us review a case of a couple that consummated a real estate deal from out of state (vacant lot) and completed the deal over the telephone. Subsequently, they built their home on the vacant lot. Later, they discovered that their home was built on a wrong lot. Evidently, the adjacent lot was their property. The owner of the mistaken property threatened a legal action and proceeded to involve the authorities. Next, the state police served this couple an order to remove their home from the lot. Clearly, this couple made a noxious mistake. First, they have spent thousands of dollars and time in the process of building the home. Second, they have spent thousands of dollars and time by tearing home down the new home and removing all the debris. Third, they will spend thousands of dollars and time to rebuild their home on the correct lot. A real estate purchase mistake, regardless of whose fault it is, is usually very exorbitant. Therefore, it is imperative for any one engaging in any type of real estate transaction to stay alert and evaluate every section of the process, prior to close a deal.

Mortgage Documents

A home buyer ready to engage in mortgage financing deal needs to pay close attention to detail such as signing multiple papers and other documents. This is because many mistakes due to predatory lending and other cheating methods may occur during the mortgage financing period. Signing the loan application papers does not obligate the borrower unless information is falsely represented. The most important signatures are the ones the buyer signs at the loan closing. The buyer chooses the transaction closing site. This can be consummated in the office of the mortgage lender, office of the title company or the home of the buyer. The responsibility of a lender and title company is to make sure that all valid documents are presented to the buyer for signatures. However, the buyer has personal obligations to make sure that the papers he/she signs are valid and meaningful. This is the most important reason why the law mandates that a borrower receives the HUD-1 closing statements at least twenty-four hours prior to the closing date.

Items contained in a mortgage document include:

1. Monthly principal and interest payments.
2. Taxes and insurance figures, if the loan is with escrow.
3. Certification of the mortgage lender with lending authorities.
4. Information of mortgage with contractual capacity.
5. Information of seller with contractual capacity.
6. Interest contained in the real property that may be mortgaged.
7. Mortgaging statement.
8. Pledge - security for payment of the debt or obligation.
9. Proper description of the premises and its surveyed boundaries.
10. Statutory covenants or agreements and clauses of mortgagor.
11. Proper execution.
12. Voluntary delivery and acceptance.
13. Other necessary disclosure documents.

The disclosure documents contain facts that the buyer must know and understand. For instance, a disclosure statement informs the buyers that they have the rights to receive the property appraisal or copies of all papers signed. Most of the rules and regulations are mandated by the government.

Mortgage Loan Closing

On the closing day, the buyer signs multiple documents. In fact, some buyers do not know or understand what they sign, why they sign and who must be present during the mortgage closing activities. It is mandated by the government, that a property buyer receives thorough explanation of every document before signing it. The final property closing activity is ready when the following persons and/or documents are present:

1. The property seller.
2. The property buyer.
3. A title company - which is the closing agency.
4. Mortgage documents – mortgage agreement papers with a HUD-1 Statement.
5. A cashier's check for the down payment, if needed,
6. A cashier's check for the closing cost, if needed,
7. A cashier's check for the appraiser, if needed,
8. All government specified disclosure documents,
9. The Lender (mortgage broker) may or may not be present at the closing. However, the mortgage broker needs to be available and answer questions from the property buyer, to correct any misunderstanding that may arise.

It is always a good practice to let the buyer read the closing statement thoroughly at least one day in advance. Thus, the buyer would know how costs and expenses are distributed, formulate questions to ask and identify how much to bring to the closing table, if needed. As previously stated, the government also directs that a copy of the HUD-1 closing statement be made available to the home buyer, at least twenty-four hours in advance. This gives a buyer time to accept or reject any or some of the figures on any document or have a change of mind about the entire deal.

CHAPTER SEVEN
Plans And Actions "After" Mortgage Financing

Monthly Mortgage Payments

A home owner plans, develops, maintains and follows through with necessary activities after mortgage financing. Some of these activities include with monthly taxes, insurance payments and mortgage payments to avoid defaults with consequential foreclosure. As agreed, a mortgage is a pledge or a loan. The essential purpose of the mortgage loan is to protect the lender, not necessarily the borrower. If a mortgagor defaults, the mortgagee (lender) may proceed to collect the balance of the debt from the property. A home owner needs to understand that even when the mortgage payments are made consistently, transfer of a real property title, from the lending institution, does not take place until the entire loan payments are complete. Until then, the home owner (home occupants) has only a title to a personal property, not a real property. Consequently, if a mortgagor dies before paying off the mortgage loan, the property will not descend to the heirs, rather, it will go to the administrator of the deceased estate. In other words, the home buyer has no asset until the loan is paid off. This is the reason why the most important document a home owner receives during a real estate transaction is the protocols concerning the loan.

Late Payments

Late payments are almost as bad as no payment. Two or more late payments will make it very difficult for a property owner to qualify for a refinancing loan. Refinancing a mortgage loan is another technique that a home owner uses to combat a foreclosure. Generally, an excuse people give for missing payments on due dates is lack of money. Other people may have problems with procrastination, forgetfulness, defiance or for some other reasons - not willing to pay the bill. For instance, in the state of Ohio there was a home mortgagor whose gross income is over a hundred thousand dollars per annum has defaults on his credit report because he owes a total of four debts amounting to twenty-eight dollars each. His mortgage loan application was rejected by three mortgage financial groups as a result of the four debts on his credit reports. The diagnosis for this applicant signals that he is unwilling to pay his bill.

Interest Payments

After purchasing a home with a mortgage loan, the mortgagor should be aware of the fact that in about two years, he or she needs to begin researching for an attractive lower interest rate. The mortgagor can refinance this same property with or without cashing out money. If there is no substantial equity in the mortgage, the home owner should refinance without cashing out money. Refinancing a property with lower interest rate helps to lower the mortgage payments. The greatest advantage of lowering interest rate is that it yields significant lower monthly payments and enhances the personality of the mortgagor. Sadly, lenders structure mortgage payments in a way that most of the monthly payments a mortgagor makes are credited to interests and only a small fraction goes to reduce the principal loan amount. The table below shows the effects of increased or decreased interest rates on real estate transactions.

Calculation of Payment Interest

Monthly, Annually and 30 – Year Periods
Principal Monthly, Annual and 30 Years Differentials
A 50 or more = one, but any less than 50 is thrown away.

1	1A	2	3	4	5	6	7
Principal Amount.	Principal Amount.	Interest Rate.	Principal Payment. Buffer/Shocker	Interest Amount.	Principal Interest.	Principal Interest.	Principal Amount.
Any amount can be used. In this example, we are using $100,000.	1 divided by a 30 Year period equals 1A. $100,000 is divided by 30 year mortgage.	A mortgage chart can be used with any interest rate.	This buffer is payment amount and each is a "constant".	The interest rate can be from 1% to 12%. I have also used 12% and seen 14%.	This payment is multiplied with one year (12 months).	The payment is multiplied with a 30 year sum (360 months).	The total amount here is the final figured amount of the mortgage sum of money.
$							
100,000	3,333	8%	278	545	823	9,876	296,280
100,000	3,333	7%	278	511	789	9,468	284,040
100,000	3,333	6%	278	478	756	9,072	272,160
100,000	3,333	5%	278	445	723	8,676	260,280
100,000	3,333	4%	278	411	689	8,268	248,040

100,000	3,333	3%	278	378	656	7,872	236,160
100,000	3,333	2%	278	345	623	7,476	224,280
100,000	3,333	1%	278	311	589	7,068	212,040
Each of these amounts is divided with a 30 year mortgage payment plan.	Each sum of $100,000 becomes $3,333 and stays constant.	An interest rate, from 8% down to 1%, is multiplied with Column 1A.	This shocker is constant, and each is added when needed.	1A x 3 + 3	Column 3 + Column 4 = Column 5, which is a monthly sum of money.	Column 5 x12 becomes a one Year period (12 months).	Column 6 x 30 = a 30 year period (360 months).

**Calculation of Payment Interest for a 1 or 2 bedroom(s) home
Monthly, Annually and 30-Year Period
(50 cents or more = $1 & 49 cents or less = thrown off)**

Column 1: It shows the principal amount borrowed. In this case, the borrowed amount is $100,000; hence, $100,000 is constant.

Column 1A: This column shows that $100,000 divides with a 30 year period = $3,333.

Column 2: It shows the interest rates, which is really acceptable for a loan from a lender.

Column 3: It is the monthly principal payments without interest. It is a buffer (shocker) or bulwark (wall) and it is constant.

Column 4: This column shows the interest amount computed with columns 1A x 2 + 3 = column 4.

Column 5. Column 5 has mortgage payments. The answer to column 5 is columns 3 + 4.

Column 6: This column is to show that column 5 multiplied by a 1 year (12 month) period. The money is too high for the mortgagors to pay.

Column 7: Column 7 is a 30 year period of mortgage. A mortgage loan can be owed 30 years (360 months).

It is now clear that, in most cases, the lenders (mortgagees) receive 2 or 2.5 percent of the interest money that is taken away from the buyers (mortgagors). Actually, the Federal Government may or should assist home buyers (mortgagors). Chapter 8 will discuss some main issues concerning to Foreclosures and Repossessions. Please refer to chapter 8, first page.

Calculation of Foreclosure and Repossession:
Please refer to chapter 8, first page = Foreclosure and Repossession:
(50 cents or more = $1 and less is thrown away.)

The above lines show column 3 (buffer), column 5 (monthly), column 6 (annually) and column 7 (30 years) to discover the Foreclosure and

Repossession amounts. Anybody can work with 8% -1%, but as of now, we shall use 8%. It is as follows:

$296,280 of column 7 is divided with 278 (column 3) = $1,066 and column 5 (monthly) is $823. Next, $1,066 − 823 = $243 for monthly.

The money wrongfully taken from buyers (mortgagors) are as below:
===

The mortgage loan periods are usually known as 30 years or 360 months
****

The first day's losses is 243 divided with 30 days = $8 (money wrongfully taken from buyers).

The first month is 243 x 1 month (1 month) = $243 (money wrongfully taken from buyers).

The first year is 243 x 12 months (one year) = $2,916 (money wrongfully taken from buyers).

The first 30 years are 243 x 30 years (30 years or 360 months) = $87,480 (money wrongfully taken from buyers).

The first 360 month period is 243 per month x 360 months = $87,480 (money wrongfully taken from buyers).

When the buyers (mortgagors) lose money from the lenders (mortgagees), they start to suffer from Foreclosure and Repossession. Very often, mortgagors would lose $243 monthly, $2,916 yearly and $87,480 for 30 years from some lenders.

Payment Incentive

Collateral is needed to finance an asset because the lender requires the loan to be secured with a previously acquired asset. In the case of a mortgage loan, the collateral could be the home/house being purchased, paid off or already purchased and mortgaged to a lender. There is another opportunity for a buyer to possess the property. A buyer who signs a loan agreement is considered to be a human collateral. The personality and dignity of the home buyer are presently tied together with the loan agreement. In the case of default, an individual cannot escape foreclosure with repossession. Lenders like to loan money to borrowers who not only have financial wealth but also manage assets properly. Indeed, a person applying for loan without any type of attractive asset to serve as collateral may not receive a loan approval. Most credit card accounts are unsecured because the recipients may not have enough wealth to pay their bills. Some other accounts are secured with both human dignity and financial wealth. In any case, it is a fact that some people need motivational technique(s) to inspire them in keeping up with their commitments.

Good motivational techniques help to build up the morale of home owners and lead home occupants to maintain efficacy and consistency in making monthly mortgage payments. One good quality of motivation is that when well done, a person gives satisfaction or feelings of accomplishment. For instance, when a farmer cultivates his farm, he derives satisfaction. It inspires him to visit his farm daily and tend to his crops daily. He does this regularly because he wants a fruitful harvest. Also, a home owner needs similar harvest. A person who purchases a house or home and obtains the monetary mortgage payment has an investment to nurture respectfully. If this exercise materializes, in a proper manner, the accomplishment is a fruitful Return on Investment (ROI). A farmer, whose farm fails, loses the crops he has in the farm but retains the farm land which is the center of his investment. On the contrary, a home owner who fails to maintain consistency with his mortgage payments loses all monetary investments on the home including the actual home which is the base of the investment. It would seem that the destiny of the farmer is better than that of the home owner because the farmer is able to retain his land while the home owner is not able to keep his home.

The diagram below explains how a person can be motivated

MOTIVATION DIAGRAM

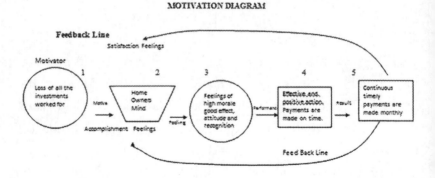

Brief Explanation

The capital outlay of a home owner increases with each periodic mortgage payment made. Furthermore, the house appreciates in value. The capital outlay yields a positive return with the equity growth of the home ROI. These growths in equity may in turn lead to possible cash-out rewards.

In box one a home owner must remain aware of the fact that a loan payment default and an eventual foreclosure with repossession is the biggest source of financial loss in the investment of a loan borrower. Thus, the consequences of loss of an investment, in box one becomes the motive for an investor.

For box two, motives hatch like eggs in the minds of home owners. The motives include default, foreclosure, and repossession, loss of capital and forfeiture of equity that will continue to develop daily in the minds of home owners. This will continuously push the investor to set money aside for taking the care of mortgage obligations.

Box three asserts that in the minds of the home owners, they recognize these motives daily and nurture feelings of high morale that encourage taking positive and effective actions toward their mortgage responsibilities.

Box four comments on the positive behavioral changes that steam from home owners. Again, box four induces strong efficacy on the part of the home owners, indicating that monthly payments are made on a timely manner, as they come due.

For box five, the success steaming from box four yields continuous good choices for the mortgagor. Thus, the effective actions in accomplishing all payment requirements and achieving goals will continue. This situation leads the investor to achieve accomplishments because a home investment with reliable and valid of ROI is intact and foreclosure with repossession is avoided.

At this point, the resulting feedbacks of lenders are feelings of satisfaction and feelings of accomplishment for the home owner. Moreover, home owners may begin to plan for more future investments. If a home owner continues to make consistent mortgage payments for at least, four years and the economy of the country is balanced, the probability of gaining decent home equity and home is very high. The home owner can request a refinance of the home with a cash-out option. The cash-out money may be reinvested in the home as a strong building block for better returns.

Investing Returns of Home Owners

A home owner in possession of equity (money) needs to research diligently where to invest the funds. A reasonable investment is one that meets the objectives and/or goals of the individual. Channels of investment selection include T-bills, Common stocks, Preferred stocks, Bonds and Real estates. Other means of investments will be listed and described later in this chapter. It is a common fact that banks and financial institutions can suffer sudden closures. Therefore, an investor needs to keep the possibility of liquidation in mind when searching for sources of investment. It is important for a person to know that investing in security also encourages the enhancement of the person's income, safety or personal status of the investor.

Security Risk

The risks involved in securities are highest for common stocks. Other securities rank in order, as shown in the risk box below

Arranged in Ascending Order towards the Highest Risk

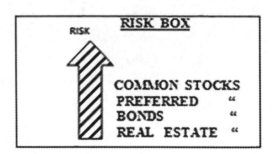

1. Common Stocks.
2. Preferred Stocks.
3. Bond Stocks.
4. Real Estate Securities/Stocks.

1. Common Stocks as Security

The risk box above requires an investor to be aware of investment risks categories. The riskiest form of investment is the common stocks, next is the preferred stocks, followed by the bonds and the lowest risk is the real estate securities. Advantages and disadvantages of each investment category are also described. Generally, most corporations ("C") issue common stocks. A share of common stock represents a share of ownership in the company, while selling the stocks. The stocks have last claim on the earnings and assets of a corporation, if other securities are issued. However, if the corporation is liquid with cash, the common stocks will be highly beneficial as they have unlimited potential for dividend payments. Moreover, common stocks could be offered the highest rewards and have the highest risk. In other words, with more money from "C" and as the profit of the corporation increases, the dividends for the common stocks go up, and as the profit of a corporation decreases, the dividends of same corporation go down. Usually, common stock owners have all voting rights in the corporation.

Disadvantages of Common Stocks
* High risk - Comparably, highest in risk among securities.
* Uncertainty - One is never sure of what the dividend will yield.
* Variability - Income pattern is unsteady.

Advantages of Common Stocks
* Good for growth purposes. Comparably, best for growth purposes.
* With time, they eventually give the highest return.

- They have all the voting rights.
- The potentiality for making money from the dividends is unlimited.

2. Preferred Stocks as Security

Preferred stocks holders earn dividends. Preferred stockholders are part-owners of the issuing corporation. The name preferred relates to preference, which means that the stocks have preference over common stocks with regard to payment of dividends. Therefore, if the corporation makes profit, preferred stockholders will be paid before the common stockholders. However, a preferred stock pays a "fixed" amount of money to its holders. Indeed, the rate of money paid is less than that of common stock because the preferred stock has less risk than the common stock. The rewards for the preferred stocks are dividends.

Advantages of Preferred Stocks
- Preferred stocks get more returns and controls than bonds.
- They are safer and have more steady income than the common stocks.
- They are paid first before the common stocks.
- They have less risk than the common stock.

Disadvantages of Preferred Stocks
- Lack of growth. Even when the profit of the issuing corporation goes up, the dividends for the preferred stocks remain the same.
- They have no voting right.
- Dividends are not guaranteed.

3. Bonds as Security

The reward for a bond is interest. A bond is a debt which, in many cases, is secured with assets of the issuing company. Each bond certificate contains relevant data which show the promise to pay a stated rate of interest for an approved time. It also comes with another promise to pay-up the principal at a specific date called maturity date. The reward for bonds is the interest amount received and bondholders are creditors.

Advantages of Bonds

- Bonds are senior securities of the issuing firm and as such have the benefits of the "*me first*" rule assuming that the issuer is making steady income.
- They are relatively safe.
- A steady income from bonds is contingent on the amount of money made by the issuer.

Disadvantages of Bonds

- Bonds lack growth.
- It is risky to allow a corporation to continue issuing more bonds without being sure of how to meet the obligations on maturity dates.
- They have no voting right in matters affecting the firm.

4. Real Estate As Security

Real estate securities are sometimes classified as bonds. As of now, real estate has gained tougher grounds to operate as separate security. Therefore, it requires separate definition. The securities in real estate are usually realized from the Real Estate

Investment Trusts (REIT). REIT is used for group ownership of an investment property. Under the provision of the new trust laws and regulations adopted by the Internal Revenue Service (IRS) on April 24, 1962, the real estate investment trusts and the regulatory standards are able to avoid corporate income taxes. This concept is based on the conditions that the trusts distribute 90% or more of the annual earnings to its shareholders and, at least, 75% of its assets must be real property. Despite the good qualities, Real Estate Securities has some unique principles.

Advantages of Real Estate Securities

- Safety - The investments are safe because real estate is usually insured.
- They yield steady income.
- Protection – These are good for the future protection of widows, widowers and children.
- The securities afford convenience and flexibility. Changes can always be made.
- Continuity - Income flows to the successors.
- Tax shelter – Real Estate taxes can be deducted from income before taxes.
- The depreciation amount (tax savings) is often subtracted before taxes.

The information above, serve as guide for home owners and other real estate property owners. Investors in the real estate industry are more able to make fruitful investment decisions and realize profitable return on the investment(s). When selecting security, home owners need to select those that best meet their goals and objectives.

Below is a table that summarizes this section. It is also a picture that may help real estate investors make their decisions and selections wisely. If an objective of the investor is to grow with security investment, buying common stocks may provide more help, followed by real estate security. The table below shows that real estate security serves best for safety purposes and has the least Risk On Investment (ROI).

Disadvantages of Real Estate Securities

- There are too many rules and regulations such as with the Internal Revenue Services (IRS) to understand and comply.
- The power of management to make decisions is limited.
- Placing 75% or more of the property on trust in fixed assets, violates the principles of liquidity which a security should possess.

Better Selection Of Investments

(For Home Owners)

Colum. 1.	Colum. 2.	Colum. 3.	Colum. 4.	Colum. 5.	Colum. 6.
Types of Securities	Income Purposes	Control Purposes	Growth Purposes	Safety Purposes	Risk On Investment
Common Stocks	Variable	100 %	Best	Least	Highest
Preferred Stocks	Steady	Steady	Variable	Good	High
Bonds	Much	None	None	Better	Little
Real Estates	Very	Some	Good	Best	Least

Brief Explanation of the Table Above

1. The first column shows the type of securities to pick from.
2. The second column shows which one to choose, if the objective for investing is to receive a steady flow of income. The best choice here is real estate (very steady income).
3. The third column shows the choice to make if the goal of the home owner is to control the issuing corporation. The best choice here is the common stocks (100% Control).
4. The fourth column shows the choice to make, if the objective is to grow with the Investment. The best choice at this time is the common stocks (best growth).
5. The fifth column shows the choice to make, if the goal is for safety purposes. The best choice here is the real estate securities (best for safety purposes).
6. The sixth column shows the magnitude of risk on each security. Also, it shows the choice the home owner needs to make, if investment risks are his concern. In this situation, a good choice is the real estate securities due to least investment risks.

Classifications of Security Issuers (Channels), (Igah, 1983).

There are hundreds of security channels available to investors. Classifications enable home buyers and owners to know or understand where to search for investment opportunities. Further, the groups included below will show home owners where to find the investment options to choose from:

1. **Classification by Security Group**

   Bonds and stocks of business or commercial corporations

   (a) Industrial companies.

   (b) Public utility companies.

   (c) Transportation companies

   (d) Securities of Financial Companies

   (e) Investment companies: bonds and shares.

   (f) Bank stocks.

   (g) Insurance company stocks.

   Securities of finance and loan companies

   (a) Government Securities

   (b) US Government obligations, including T-bills.

   (c) State and municipal bonds.

   (d) Securities of foreign governments.

2. **Classification by Deposit Group**

   (a) Postal Savings deposit.

   (b) Savings deposits in the commercial banks.

   (c) Deposits in mutual savings banks.

   (d) Accounts in savings and loans associations.

   (e) Shares in the credit unions.

   (f) Deposits in the industrial banks.

3. **Classification by Insurance and Retirement Groups**

   (a) Life insurance.

   (b) Annuities: fixed and variable.

   (c) Government retirement plans - social security.

   (d) Private retirement plan.

4. **Classification by Real Estate Group**
   Real Estate Mortgages and Securities
   (a) Real estate property.
   (b) Designed for income.
   (c) Designed for occupancy.

5. **Classification by Business Group**
   (a) Investor status.
   (b) Security.
   (c) Maturity features.
   (d) Degree of marketability.
   (e) Tax status.
   (f) Degree of management required.
   (g) Degree of risk.
   (h) Degree of protection against price changes.

6. **Public Utilities Include the Following**
   (a) Electric light and power.
   (b) Gas.
   (c) Gas transmission.
   (d) Telephone.
   (e) Water.
   (f) Local transit.

7. **Transportation Include the Following**
   (a) Railroads or Railways.
   (b) Airways.
   (c) Waterways.
   (d) Other interurban transportation modes.
   (Igah 1983), (Jordan & Dowgall 1960).

CHAPTER EIGHT
Foreclosure Causes And Repossession Pains

A. DESCRIPTION

1. Chapter eight shows that lenders (mortgagees) foreclose home owners (mortgagors) with false home payments. When a mortgagor defaults on mortgage payments, the lender (mortgagee) activates an eviction notice against the mortgagor. Thereafter, a court action approves that the mortgagee can remove the mortgagor from his or her property. For this reason, the mortgagee legally forecloses the mortgagor from the property. Henceforth, the mortgagor suffers from home foreclosure, while searching for another home. Unfortunately, a court sheriff legally sends the mortgagor and his family, if any, out to no other shelter. Next, the mortgagor starts to suffer from repossession.

2. Property Foreclosure Causes

Property Repossession Pains
Foreclosure Causes - Controllable and Uncontrollable.

• Property and Foreclosure Causes

A real estate foreclosure occurs when a mortgage lender files legal action to nullify a mortgage loan agreement made with a borrower. The purpose of this action is to cancel the present mortgage agreement, remove the current owner(s) or occupant(s) from the home and retitle the property to the mortgage lender. The lender may at this point, proceed to sell the property to a new borrower. Hopefully, the sales proceed will be enough to cover the remaining balance of the loan. One core reason for a mortgage lender to initiate a foreclosure action is because the property owner no longer makes consistent mortgage payments on maturity dates.

• Property Repossession Pains

Repossession is the lender's removal of property and its title against the home owner. Therefore, the home owner (mortgagor) and his or her family will try to recover their mortgaged property. Due to government interventions, some home owners are still living in homes that are going through foreclosures. In this case, it is called foreclosure without repossession. Studies show that many mortgage lenders prefer foreclosure with consequential repossession. Since repossessions are important factors for foreclosures, foreclosure of properties precede repossessions, except if the government intervenes or the judge arbitrates.

• Foreclosure Causes - Controllable and Uncontrollable.

The controllable and uncontrollable foreclosure with repossession, are preventable and unpreventable to real estate foreclosure with repossession.

Controllable – Foreclosure with Repossession Session

The controllable causes of foreclosures are preventable and help to avoid foreclosures with repossessions. Controllable causes are those that mortgagors are able to resolve. People often say that "prevention is always better than cure". Foreclosure causes are controllable because mortgagors can settle and prevent problems with their real estate lenders. Thus, foreclosure causes are said to be controllable because mortgagors and mortgagees can work corporately together and prevent the problems. Some foreclosure problems arise from multiple predatory lending techniques created by mortgagees against their mortgagors. However, if a home owner lives in the same home for about two or more years and does not default on mortgage payments, it is more likely that the mortgagor will have minimal or no problem with the lending practice. Actually, some home owners make correct and consistent mortgage payments, for at least five to twenty years and did not avoid foreclosures with repossessions. Finally, when a controllable problem is not settled with both mortgagor and mortgagee, the mortgagor suffers from foreclosure and/or repossession.

Uncontrollable

The uncontrollable causes of foreclosures with or without repossessions are unpreventable. Sometimes, mortgage owners do not understand the uncontrollable causes of foreclosures. For instance, if a mortgagor becomes unemployed the result may be a lack of money to pay mortgage bills. Further, it will be more difficult for the lenders (mortgagees) to work cooperatively with the mortgagors. Mortgagors can control these issues by effectively applying the following factors: (a) Create a proficient plan to tackle problems before they happen, (b) Adopt helpful actions that will lead to successful problem solving, (c) Use valuable techniques to resolve any pending or foreseeable problem and (d) Utilize resourceful negotiation skills when dealing with the mortgagee and other related entities.

- **Instruction of Controllable and Uncontrollable Causes**

    - **Default of mortgage agreement:** An evasion of a mortgage loan, damage to property or violation of any other core constraint in the mortgage contract is a default of mortgage agreement. In order to reverse an uncontrollable factor and make it controllable, a home owner has to make good use of the four listed uncontrollable factors described in the paragraphs above.

    - **Violation of the law:** A property owner who in any manner, does not comply with the laws of the land, invites legal actions. The same owner will be held responsible for the consequences the law permits. The lender may file a foreclosure action in an attempt to recover the money loaned on the property, especially, if the mortgage payments have been violated.

    - **Abandonment:** There are many reasons why properties are abandoned. For instance, the home owner can relocate to another geographical location and stop maintaining the home. Other reasons for abandoning homes or properties include mortgagor's health issues (chronic illnesses), imprisonments, unemployment and/or death. In each case, the concerned lender may start a foreclosure action. The home owner could avoid abandonment by selling or transferring the property to a buyer. Nowadays, more home buyers use the short-sale options to discontinue with the ownership of the buildings.

B. REMEDIES OR MITIGATIONS TO SOLUTION FOR FORECLOSURE WITH REPOSSESSION PAINS

Solutions for Foreclosures with Repossessions

(1) Remedies or Mitigations for False Money Reservations – Loan Addition

(2) Remedies or Mitigations for False Payments - Foreclosure and Repossession

(3) Remedies or Medications for Interest Rates - Foreclosure and Repossession

(4) Remedies or Mitigations for refund to mortgagors with previous interest payments.

1. REMEDIES or MITIGATIONS FOR FALSE MONEY RESERVATION – LOAN ADDITION

MORTGAGE PAYMENTS FOR NEWLY FAIR ACTIONS

Sometimes, mortgage loans are increased with additional money against home owners (mortgagors). The extra loan money is added to the mortgagors' monthly home payments. In the case of unforeseen foreclosure with repossession, lenders will use the extra money to mitigate loses. It is wrong when lenders do not refund the extra money, to the mortgagors, when they are consistent with their monthly mortgage payments, for many years. Unfortunately, when home owners find themselves in a difficult financial situation, they suffer foreclosure with/or repossession and without receiving the extra money paid towards their monthly mortgage bills. Due to this wrong doing and/or ignorance, home owners have suffered homelessness, hunger, and financial losses for years. This condition is still happening today.

With foreclosure and/or with repossession, mortgagors do not receive their money. With a cancelled home payment, money should be sent to the mortgagor. An example method is as follows:

For Example

The home purchase value	=	$ 124,000
The mortgage loan amount	=	100,000
The Down – payment amount	=	24,000
With foreclosure, the mortgage loan balance	=	96,000
The home owner paid $750 monthly for 5 years and the extra $10,000 is for others.	=	54,000

($750 monthly = $9,000 for each year, for 5 years = $45,000 paid to lenders. With the foreclosure the home owner received $4,000 and lender has taken the other $50,000 as interest rates. This is the reason why the home owner wonders why he has only $4,000 from $54,000. The lender owes his loan balance of ($100,000 - 4,000) $96,000. Unfortunately, the home owner cannot do anything about this, not even with the court actions

2. REMEDIES OR MITIGATION FOR FALSE PAYMENTS
MORTGAGE PAYMENTS FOR NEWLY FAIR ACTIONS

According to research, lenders (mortgagees) reserve extra cost of property payments belonging to home owners (mortgagors)

and lenders refused to give the money to the mortgagees. Wrong monetary stolen is needed to loose the property payments, loose the property interests, loose the down-payments, loose the foreclosed properties and other financial punishments, such as:

(i)   Mortgagees find ways (past, current and future) to receive money from false property payments.

(ii) Mortgagors have suffered and continued to suffer false foreclosures with repossessions.

(iii) Mortgagors do not know how to ask or discover the best way to work with mortgage property payments.

(iv) Federal, State and Local governments should require to help the mortgagees.

(v)   Also, lenders should help mortgagees to utilize reasonable property payments.

3. REMEDIES OR MITIGATIONS

INTEREST RATES MORTGAGE PAYMENTS FOR NEWLY FOR FAIR ACTIONS

Foreclosures with repossessions have existed as a result of interest rates on property loans. This problem can be corrected with high interest rate payment on mortgage loans. Actually, the estate lenders submit mortgage loans with different sizes of interest rates.

The citizens of this country are pleading to all Federal, State and Local governments to restore fair and better mortgage interest amounts by approving the following:

Loans' Interest rates paid by mortgagees, shall be 4% at all times.

(i)   With the sharing of the 4% interest rates, each lender (mortgagee) shall receive 2% interest rates and each home owner (mortgagor) shall have the remaining 2% interest rates.

(ii)   The 2% interest rate with a mortgagee receives a stand as enough and normal.

(iii)   The 2% interest rate with a mortgagor receives a stand as enough and normal. The money will be deposited in an interest bearing savings account of a financial institution, preferably with the Attorney General Bank.

(iv)   Mortgage loans with interest rates higher or lower than the 4% (2% and 2%), will be a violation of the laws of Federal, State and local governments.

(v)   If a home owner receives foreclosure with/or without repossession, the Attorney General Bank will send the realized 2% money to the home's mortgagor.

(vi)   If a home owner completes his or her mortgage loan fully, all the money yielded from the 2% interest rates will be dispatched to him or her from the bank.

(vii)   If a mortgagor qualifies for the Reversal Mortgage System, both the 2% interest rates with the mortgagee and the 2% interest rate with the mortgagor must be cancelled. The earlier 2% interest money should be refunded to the mortgagor.

(viii) With down-payment fund, the mortgagee should send back the money to the mortgagor going through foreclosure with/or without repossession.

(ix) During the foreclosure with/or without repossession, a resold property with the back loan payment, should be reconciled and profits go to the mortgagor.

Interest Rate Payments Versus Social Security Payments

Research has shown that most mortgagors are younger than sixty-five years old; hence they may not receive social security payments. Therefore, mortgagors with foreclosures or/with repossessions, will not be old enough to receive retirement funds but they can receive their 2% interest rates funds. The remedies for home owners are: rental houses - instead of homelessness, food and clothes - instead of hunger and home necessities - instead of acute poverty.

4. REMEDIES FOR MITIGATIONS FOR CORRECTION.

PAST PAYMENTS WITH PREVIOUS PAYMENTS
TO MORTGAGORS FOR APPROVAL
FROM FEDERAL GOVERNMENT

Often, a depressed economy is mostly blamed for people losing their jobs. In a depressed economy, more people file for bankruptcy, which in turn, multiplies their problems. As a result of filing bankruptcies and foreclosures, many affluent or middle class families presently are classified as lower SES families with very little resources to sustain their lifestyles. Some of the consequences stand from the fact that hard working people continue to seek supports from other citizens, businesses and government programs. It is necessary to find a way to help mortgagors with their payments. Somebody has to find a way to take care of these problems.

Mortgagors have suffered from foreclosure causes and/or repossession pains. The author shows how to take care of mortgagors with previous foreclosure and/or repossession. Therefore, lenders, citizens and Governments can take care of previous mortgagors as follows:

(i) A mortgagor of a foreclosed property, who has paid interest rates with monthly payments for one to three years, should receive a refund of 20% of previously made interest rates with monthly payments. However, a mortgagor who is legally recognized as a person with disability should receive a refund of 25% of the previously made interest rate payments.

(ii) A mortgagor of a foreclosed property, who has made interest rates with monthly payments for over three years and not more than six years, should receive a refund of 25% of previously made interest rates with monthly payments. However, a mortgagor who is legally recognized as a person with disability should receive a refund of 30% of previously made interest rate payments.

(iii) A mortgagor of a foreclosed property, who has made interest rates with monthly payments for over six years but not more than 10 years, should receive a refund of 30% of previously made interest rates with monthly payments. However, if a mortgagor is legally documented as a person with disability, he or she should receive a refund of 35% from the payments made earlier.

(iv) A mortgagor, whose property is foreclosed but has made consistent monthly interest payments for over 10 years, should receive a refund of 40% from the interest payments formerly made on each of the mortgage payments.

However, if the mortgagor is legally established as a person with disability, he or she should receive a refund of 45% from the mortgage payments previously made.

(v) Most importantly, these lenders keep 100% of property that engages in foreclosure or repossession activities. Renovating a property minimally, assists a lender to sell the house for more than its worth. Due to the appreciation in value of the home and especially in a flourishing economy, the lenders stand to realize a price that exceeds the initial loan amount borrowed. Note that in case of a decline in property sale, the same lender is protected by different insurance programs and the mortgagor maintains the all the insurance payments

C. IMMEDIATE AND REMOTE CAUSES

(Foreclosure Causes with Repossession Pains)

The uncontrollable causes of foreclosure with repossession are further divided into "immediate" and "remote" causes. The immediate causes are recent activities that occur in the short run (one year or less) while the remote causes have existed in the long run (more than one year). It is worth remarking that the uncontrollable factors are the main reasons of foreclosure with repossession. It is good to remember that foreclosure happens first before repossession and repossession does not happen without a foreclosure.

Immediate Causes (Foreclosure with Repossession Pains)

(1) Unemployment and/or poor economy.

(2) Default in mortgage payments.

    (3) Excessive mortgage payments

    (4) Ways to avoid foreclosure.

    (5) Consequences of foreclosure with repossession

        (a) Homelessness

        (b) Acute Poverty

        (c) Hopeless Hunger

        (d) Psycho-Social.

    (6) Possible Foreclosure with Repossession Remedies.

    (7) Prime Rate.

1. Unemployment and or Poor Economy

Foreclosure with repossession of the property has been in existence for many years and intensifies during periods of poor and depressed economy. Some serious problems that aggravate default payments are job lay-offs, sicknesses, accidental injuries, family issues, emotional conditioning and/or death. A mortgagor who suddenly becomes unemployed will have difficulties paying the maturing monthly mortgage bill. The unemployment compensation of money for a qualified person, takes some weeks or months to be processed and sent to the person. Generally, the compensation of money is marginal and not enough to cover the person's mortgage and other pressing necessities. Meanwhile, the mortgagor will continue with job search. When the economy of a country, such as the USA, descends from bad to worse, human survival goes from harder to hardest. A person in a downward type of economy is considered very lucky to find any type of employment. The USA real estate industry has suffered depressed economy since the year of 2006 and more people have embraced bankruptcies. Consequently, many home owners or occupants have lost their homes to foreclosures and/ or repossessions. Therefore, a poor, depressed or recessed economy leads to a high level of unemployment. This, in turn, causes significant defaults with loan payments.

2. Default in Mortgage Payments

Default may lead to foreclosures. Usually, the mortgage lender initiates a court action to evict the mortgage borrower who is in fault of mortgage payments. Generally, a repossession of property occurs after the due process protocols of a court action. Legally, the court permits the lender to take over the complete ownership of the property. Therefore, default of mortgage payments results in home or house foreclosure and repossession. Legal action forces a borrower and other residents, if any, in the home to physically vacate the property, (on a specified date) on their own volition or face forceful eviction, resulting from the court action.

Tips to Help Control Defaults in Payment Schedule

- A proper negotiation process with lenders will terminate the foreclosure actions.
- When the property is refinanced, the mortgage lender ends the action.
- Financing a lower cost of home or move into a new home before foreclosure activities begin.

3. Excessive Mortgage Payments

A mortgagee, who defaults on a tenancy agreement, receives no monetary refunds from the owner of the house, unless the tenant left some conditional contingent security deposit funds with the mortgagor. The mortgagor returns the deposit to the tenant on the condition that the tenant did not breech the tenancy agreement such as, owing back rent or inflicting serious damage on the property. When the rent or any part of the rented property becomes uncomfortable or unbearable to the tenant, they can rent and transfer to a more promising property becomes imminent. Contrarily, a mortgagee is tied down to a mortgage contract.

Similarly, home owners pay excess bills to lenders and do not receive reimbursements of any amount of money, previously paid. Real estate lenders are know to inflate interest rates, which they charge to the borrowers, therefore, the excess money in the possession of these lenders should go back to the home owners, when all settlements are completed (Guttentag & Roitburg, 1986). Mortgagors incur multiple over lapping funds through multiple insurances and interest payments that they make during mortgage transactions.

4.   Ways to Avoid Foreclosure

Foreclosure is the biggest threats to real estate home owners and the industry. Foreclosure generates problems such as homelessness, low self-worth, hunger and bad credit. The best technique that helps avoid foreclosure is to maintain consistent mortgage payments. However, when there is a threat of foreclosure, the mortgagor may transfer the mortgage to another lender and rescue the property. This practice is called refinancing. Another good idea is to check all signed documents concerning the property to make sure that all are valid. If a document is not valid, a law suit can be filled against the lender. A court appointed Judge may order the lender to make the necessary corrections and restart the mortgage. A home buyer may request an extension of time as well as a lower interest rate. A lender may not only grant this request but also extend the loan pay-off dates. A thirty-year loan can be stretched to forty years. The accomplishment of any or all of the above requests will result in lower monthly payments. The lower monthly payments will, assist the buyer in avoiding payment defaults and foreclosure. It is imperative that any property buyer should work with basic common sense techniques to defeat foreclosure. Researchers agree with these ideas. A mortgagor facing a foreclosure may make use of the powers of the Regulation Z that yields the Truth in Lending (TIL) documents. A copy of the documents, as listed below, may be taken to a real estate expert for examination. If an error is found, a legal action can be filed to nullify the foreclosure, Laurence Adams (1986).

Documents to Examine Include:

- Title fees.
- Interest on the mortgage.
- Closing or settlement cost.
- Loan fee.
- Buy-down fees.
- Appraisal fees charged
- Interest locking fees.
- Insurance premium paid or paying monthly.
- Premiums for property insurance.
- Origination fee.
- Any other service charges.

The legal system requires lenders to fully disclose all finance costs. If an omission or discrepancy is discovered, it could be because the mortgagee wrongly included a cost in the Annual

Percentage Rate (APR). On the other hand, the lender could have mistakenly omitted necessary data, which need to be included, in the disclosure documents. If any of these occurs, the property buyer has a legal claim to present to the court and the foreclosure may be delayed or cancelled.

5. Consequences of Foreclosure with Repossession

People sometimes say that a disappointment can be a blessing in disguise. A foreclosure with repossession makes it more difficult for a victim to sense a blessing in disguise. The effected home owners suffer different types of consequences. The worst consequences include problems like homelessness, acute poverty, hunger, financial and psycho-social problems.

(i) Homelessness

In the case of foreclosure with repossession, the lender takes over the ownership of the property concerned. The court designates a sheriff to legally remove the resident/purchaser and/ or family from the repossessed home. This type of sheriff action happens every day in this country. Consequently, families are thrown out of their homes to go and find shelter some where else. Next, these families become homeless and need help from the public or government agencies.

Many home owners that face foreclosures have children. These children are usually confused as they may not understand why they must vacate their homes. The media and other story channels bring daily awareness to these shocking activities. Further, pictures of non-profit and profit making programs, bring awareness to the types of temporary homes they offer to qualified disadvantaged persons. Likewise, some victims use their automobiles, abandoned or vacant homes or tents to serve as their new homes.

(ii) Acute Poverty

Very often, when home owners or occupants suddenly loose their jobs, their life styles descend from higher to lower class. Some home owners may not have access to a retirement accounts or asset because the holders of these funds are either broke or gone into bankruptcies. Poverty is a critical problem. Poverty creates psycho-social problems such as poor morale, shame, guilt and loss of status in the community. In some cases, the individual ceases from communicating with friends, attending social gatherings and / or attending important community meetings. Organizations such as churches have programs that assist people to fight against poverty and hunger. A section from a Catholic Church Telegraph states: "Is not this the fast that I choose … Is it not to share your bread with the hunger and bring the homeless poor into your house?" Continuing, the telegraph provides the following data:

$ 1,000 keeps the heat and lights on for six families.

$ 500 saves a family from becoming homeless.

$ 250 gives rescue inhalers to seven Charitable Pharmacy patients suffering from asthma.

$ 100 gives a soft warm bed to a child sleeping on a cold floor.

$ 50 feeds a family of four for a week.

"Society of Saint Vincent de Paul." (2013).

(iii) Hunger

There are two types of hunger. The first is periodic hunger, which occurs when a person is periodically hungry because he or she stays busy and postpones eating for lunch and dinner time. Moreover, some people must wait for lunch time or quitting time to eat, if they are engaged in a job, school, home, appointment or training environment. These people are hopeful that at a certain time, they will be able to eat their meal properly and in relaxed environment. The second type of hunger is hopeless hunger. This occurs when foreclosure victims, for example, have no idea of what to eat, when to eat or where to find food. At this point, hopelessness steps in as they have no hope of going home and no hope of when their problems will end or mitigate. A worst case scenario is if the victims have underage children who do not understand the condition of thinks. When victims vacate their homes, as a result of foreclosures, they suffer homelessness, acute poverty and /or hopeless hunger.

(iv) Psychosocial Problems

Victims of real estate foreclosure suffer different levels of psychosocial problems. When a mortgagor that maintains a decent job and living a comfortable lifestyle becomes unemployed, the probable consequence is likely to be the loss of the family home. This will cause this mortgagor and family to descend to a lower social class rating in both his or her family system and the society. He/she may suffer from guilt, shame or become withdrawn from multiple social gatherings in the community.

6. Possible Foreclosure with Repossession Remedies

Solving a foreclosure issue requires that everyone maintains an open mind. A practical remedy to stop the exploitation of mortgagors is for the real estate industry to collaborate with other related businesses. Each entity must agree to settle for an agreed and fair percentage in profit, as opposed to each professional remaining autonomous where profit margin is concerned. It is certain that real estate lenders must have interest payments in order to make some type of profit for the maintenance of their staff and other business overheads. Fair interest rate and fair profit must replace excessive interest payments, penalty charges, profits, bonuses and other types of exaggerated payments. If mortgage interest rate is fairly structured, such as prime rate plus two, a home owner or occupant will be more able to save money which may be used to pay rent for another property in the case of an unforeseeable foreclosure. Thus, if mortgage payments are reasonably low, a foreclosure is not likely to result because the home owners will find it easier to move forward with the mortgage payments, as contracted.

7. Prime Rate

It is noted earlier, that although some citizens are "homeless", all citizens of this country live in different types of shelters. Some to these shelters are homes, houses, dormitories, tents, under bridges and transportation vehicles. Nevertheless, most people reside in homes or houses. This means that all people are either home/house owners or potential home/house owners. A democratic country belongs to her citizens. Therefore, the citizens have the responsibility of electing government officials they deem fit to lead, direct, serve, protect, develop and maintain their assets to a significant degree. The elevation of mortgage interest rates takes away money and homes from the same citizens the government is believed to safeguard. Money and/or real estate properties are core assets and livelihood of citizens. Since people must live in homes or houses, they will continue to purchase real estate properties. While interrogating people for the purposes of writing this book, a home owner states that her most important goal is to make certain that the government is working towards the betterment of her home, animals and saved up money because she is not able to live without owning these assets. Further, mortgagees must pay the fees and the premiums for their own insurance protection as opposed to adding the fees to the contract of the mortgagees.

The Home Protection Act (HPA) needs to be reviewed and amended. If all stipulations in this section are examined closely and adopted, foreclosures with repossessions pains, will be stopped or reduced significantly

D. Remote Causes (Foreclosure with Repossession Pains)

(1) Uneven Mortgage interest rates.
(2) Overly collection of interest, other fees and penalties.
(3) Unnecessary cheating.
(4) Undue insurance premiums Against House Owners.
(5) Gross Injustice Against Real Estate Buyers & Home Owners
(6) Persistent frauds in the real estate industry.

1. Uneven Mortgage Interest Rates

The mortgage interest rates are excessively high and mostly because they are governed by some types of greed surrounding the real estate industry. However, interest payments are sometimes overly charged against borrowers. The recipients of interest rates make a lot of money, including paychecks and bonuses. Sometimes, people say that the existing mortgage interest rate of four to six per cent is historically high. On the other hand, past experiences show that interest rates have been overwhelmingly outrageous in the real estate industry. In the real estate discipline, a normal profit is a reward but an excessive profit is a rip off or theft. In a depressed economy, the Federal Government prime rate is zero. Therefore, any interest rate higher than four per cent (2% = lender and 2% = mortgagors) is usually aimed at excessive profit. Prime rate is the interest rate that the Federal government may negotiate with mortgage lenders or financial institutions. Further, the Federal government may need to dictate when lenders borrow the money they lend to citizens or borrowers. Unjust mortgage interest rate is the most significant cause of foreclosures with or without repossessions. This is the main reason why an entity, like the federal government, would needs to correct the mortgage interest rates. In fact, all levels of interest rates greater than prime plus four (2% + 2%) are too high and frequently will lead to unfair profiteering. Of course, the Federal government is the only entity that prints money. The congress may install justice to make them prevent mortgage lenders from charging interest rate of no more than prime plus four per cent. Already, some companies or corporations are abiding by the principles of "fair profit." Also, during a time of poor, depressed or mismanaged economy, significant numbers of hard working citizens loose their jobs and homes. It is necessary to understand that if the interest rate is limited to prime plus four, a lot of real estate foreclosures in this country would have been avoided. Unfortunately, most mortgage loans are structured in a way that the first 20 years are mostly interest payments. Thus, when a mortgagor pays monthly mortgage loan, only about 18% – 24% is credited to the principal of the mortgage loan. The remaining percentages of the money are retained as interest payments and profits. The principal is the loan money with no interest, hence the remaining loan money will be (100% - 24%) 76%. This is a major reason why, mortgagors who make genuine mortgage payments, for many years, are surprised to note that the outstanding balance of their loans are (76%) still very high. In view of this, mortgagors wonder where most of the money they pay as monthly mortgage bill is for years. With such a huge loan balance, the court approves a foreclosure and repossession against the property. Conceivably, the legal system needs to learn more about how to intervene or interfere in any false loan of real estate industry. The interest rates of 2% to lender and 2% to homeowners are explained above.

2. Overly Collection of Interest Fees, Other Fees and Penalty

Many lenders or investors claim that high interest rates go to protect against the risks of absent mortgage payments. This claim is wrong because lenders do not know which borrowers will default. Studies show that mortgage borrowers wrongly pay for defaults in two primary ways. The first is the compulsory risk premium on interest rates. Risk premium is an interest rate increment above the prime rate loan agreement. Mortgagees receive this fund from mortgagors as part as income and as opposed to reserving same payment to cover risk emergencies. A second weakness of interest rate risk premium system is that the excess money collected is used and not on actual losses of borrowers. Instead, these excess interest rates are used to cover the return the investors believe to compensate for the risk of going broke such as salaries and bonuses, for lenders. Such premiums are substantially higher than the premiums based on actual work experiences. Indeed, mortgage lenders can charge higher interest rates as shields for risks that are based on opinions of the lenders. Further, this practice is damaging to home owners because high interest rates increase their monthly mortgage payments. Some of these complications involve legal orders, other fees, default in current mortgage payments, loss of equity built on property, foreclosures and /or repossessions of homes, previously invested in the property over the years, loss of prestige, loss of freedom and lack of trust in the overall real estate system.

3. Unnecessary Cheating

A significant amount of money belonging to borrowers (home owners) are collectively put together and then charged as fees and penalties against home owners. Sometimes, houses in foreclosure sell at prices much higher than the outstanding loan balance. Usually, a home owner going through an eviction process against them suffers much with foreclosure and repossession pains. Apparently, a genuine audit system designed to protect borrowers, is needed to help in understanding how the excess money mentioned, help the real estate industry. For instance, a letter from a National Bank to a mortgagor who has vacated her home because she could no longer afford her mortgage payments, demanded full omitted mortgage payments within ten days after receiving the letter or the home would be boarded-up for security purposes, at the expense of the borrower. Further, same letter noted that the security boarding exercise would protect the mutual interest of the mortgage lender and the mortgage borrower. Since this bank seems to be concerned about mutual interest in the property, the question remains on why the borrower is the only entity responsible for all the expense involving the security costs. This borrower will receive nothing of value from the sale of her previously managed home as a result of foreclosure. Thus, citizens need to contact their congress men, congress women and other qualified government officials, about issues that continue to plague the real estate industry.

4. Unjust Insurance Premiums-Against Home Owners

(i) Sometimes, people say that justice is blind. The equitable payment of the insurance costs in mortgage financing is an area where justice can be said to be blind. Unfortunately, real estate officials including government representatives do not see a need to take necessary actions in fixing problems in this area. At the closing of real estate transactions, the potential property buyers often wonder why closing costs are very high. Some reasons for these high costs are blamed on the adding and the lumping of multiple unnecessary financial points. A mortgage loan borrower, for instance, is responsible for five different insurance payments which swells the closing cost. The five insurance payments are: Hazard Insurance (HI), Mortgage Insurance Protection (MIP), the Title Insurance for the lender, and Title Insurance for the Borrower and the Flood Insurance. These insurance categories are explained below.

(ii) Hazard Insurance, (HI)

Hazard insurance protects against risks for major damages to a property. For instance, if a house incurs a major damage, the HI will pay, at least, the loan amount to the mortgage lender. The cost of hazard insurance is usually included in the mortgage closing cost. After closing, it is added to the monthly mortgage payments by the home owners.

Mortgage Insurance Protection, (MIP). Private Mortgage Insurance, (PMI) Mortgage Protection Insurance (MIP) is the money that mortgage borrowers pay to protect the lenders of the Federal Housing Administration (FHA) loans. This insurance protects the mortgage lenders against mortgage defaults or foreclosures. All FHA mortgage loans are insured up to 97% of the total mortgage loan a person requests. A mortgagor, who is insured for about 97%, explains that in the case of a default or foreclosure, the FHA will cover up to about 97 % of the outstanding loan balance. If the FHA mortgage insurance is 97% or 96.5%, it explains that the borrower has the responsibility of paying, a down- payment of, 3% or 3.5% of the total loan amount or forfeit the loan. The reason for this action is to protect the mortgage lender at a range closer to 100%. The 97% protection from the FHA and the 3% from the loan borrower add up to 100%. In fact, the down payment for the loan borrower has increased from 3% to 3.5%, in the past few years. In view of this, the down payment for a mortgage loan of $100,000 is $3,500 and for $98,100 is $3,433.50. The questions most people ask are whose money is protected? Whose investment is protected? Whose profit is protected? If a default or foreclosure occurs, who gains by receiving all the insurance proceeds? When a foreclosure occurs on a property, the mortgage lender receives the entire money the borrower invested in the property.

Private Mortgage Insurance (PMI) is the private (non-government) insurance which home borrowers pay when their conventional loans are lower than 80% of the appraisal value. A significant purpose of this insurance is to protect mortgage lenders against any loss in a case of default or foreclosure. The two insurance programs of PMI and MIP are very similar except that MIP is government Insurance and PMI is for non-governmental loans. Usually, lenders include a lump of money in the closing cost as MIP or PMI which the borrowers must pay. Nevertheless, the same borrowers who pay the monthly premiums of MIP or PMI are not protected by any of these insurance programs. When a home forecloses, the home owners do not receive any benefit or any share from any of the insurance proceeds.

(iii)   Title Insurance for the Lender (TIL)

The title insurance company is the only entity that the law empowers to perform mortgage loan closings. The legal duties of a title company is to make sure that the house being sold is free of liens except the lender, a seller is the rightful owner or has an agent with a power of attorney, other necessary bindings and findings are legal and satisfactory. Sometimes, a title company may, inadvertently, fail to bring up a valid lien on a house listed for sale. After the house sales, the lien holder retains a legal first claim on the property which is a liability to the lender who financed the house. The liability is discovered after the sale of the property. At this point, the title insurance for the mortgage lender corrects the situation for the home owner to make them to the payments to lender. The borrower receives nothing from the insurance payments. Further, the borrower makes monthly payments towards the insurance premium or forfeits the loan.

(iv)   Title Insurance for the Borrower (TIB)

TIB pays liability costs a borrower is responsibility for paying. Many borrowers, for some reason, elect to buy the TIB insurance even though, the lenders do not cost any of the lost funds. However, if a borrower accepts the TIB, the cost is also added to the closing cost of this borrower. All of these variables contribute to the reason why closing cost is high.

(v)   Flood Insurance for the Lender (FIL)

Flood insurance protects a house against flood (water) emergencies. This insurance protects properties located in marked flood zones. Unfortunately, the hazard insurance does not cover flood damages until mortgagors pay for them. If a house is destroyed by flood, the flood insurance pays mortgagors the cost of the damages and the proceeds go to the mortgage lenders. Again, nothing goes to the mortgage borrower for the protection of the home investments. Therefore, home buyers are responsible for four different insurance premiums for their lenders.

5.   Gross Injustice against Real Estate Buyers & Home Owners

Real estate lenders do not need to impose money to protect against home owners. The four different types of mortgage insurance programs are paid by the borrowers, as described earlier. The mortgagees receive all property money and home owners (borrowers) pay for all property requirements. Home owners (mortgagors) are required to make such payment as hazard insurance, mortgage insurance protection, monthly payments, title insurance, false penalties with fees, home taxes, excessive interest rates and others. The items shown above are used to take care of lenders (mortgagees) but all of them are paid by the mortgagors. With all the payments shown above, luxurious assets can be as follows:

i   Live with their fantastic homes.

ii   Own their beautiful vehicles.

iii   Purchase more homes in different States.

iv   Acquire their private jets and/or aircrafts

v   Own fanciful boats and yachts.

vi   Contribute more money to friends.

vii   Enough to start small and/or large businesses enterprises.

ix   Increase employment by hiring more friends.

x   Mortgagors have none of the above.

It should be remembered that both homes and mortgage loans belong to the financial lenders. The home owners simply occupy and pay home money to lenders who are the legal property owners. Mortgagors do not become owners of their homes until their entire mortgage loans are fully paid. Therefore, lenders, who are legal owners, need to be responsible for the insurance protection costs.

6. Persistent Frauds in the Real Estate Industry

When a home owner suffers from fraud activities, the mortgage lender initiates a foreclosure action, but the same fraud activities being suffered on the mortgagors are done by the mortgage lenders. However, a home buyer who research diligently before purchasing a real estate property will find it much easier to detect an action. Presently, the government encourages any one who witnesses any type of fraud activity to report the action to the law authorities. Frauds can be classified as uncontrollable actions, foreclosure causes and repossession pains.

CHAPTER NINE
Accommodation Program
- Problem Mitigation

The solution suggested in chapter seven seems to be adequate with the diagrams but meanwhile, we can look for a way to control the problem of accommodation. Obviously, foreclosure with repossession is not a remedy instead, it creates bigger difficulties. They are like certain diseases, such as diabetes and high blood pressure that have no cure. Likewise, a suitable prescription will help to control the foreclosure problem. Like the diseases, the foreclosure with repossession has been here for many years and is going nowhere. Since it is going nowhere, it makes sense to structure a way to accommodate it. Although the accommodation program is not a complete solution, it will, at least, mitigate the problem effects. So far, some lenders are trying the programs which seem to be failing. One of them is based on offering monetary rewards to anybody willing to buy a foreclosed unit while the other one is based on lowering the prices of foreclosed homes and taking a light or heavy loss.

Unfortunately, most of the foreclosed houses are in very poor or damaged conditions and will cost thousands of dollars to accomplish the repairs. If people look for reasonable homes, they move shy away from houses that are poorly maintained. On the other hand, many foreclosure advisory entities have opened awake in different parts of the country and they tell the victims what they already know. Their best advice to the victims is to call and negotiate with the mortgagee or to see a lawyer. If a poor victim has money to engage a lawyer and pay other legal fees, he or she would have been able to pay the mortgage bills and abate the foreclosure. Besides, mortgage agreements are so lengthy and thorough that a lawyer cannot shorten or nullify them. So, what is the point? The victim has only waste their time. Actually, the society needs a program to reshuffle the mortgage financing and limits or control the prevalent foreclosures with repossessions.

REAL ESTATE FORECLOSURE ACCOMMODATION PROGRAM (REFA) PROGRAM F O R "RESSHUFFLED MORTGAGE FINANCING" (RMF)

Reshuffled Mortgage Financing (RMF) is the outcomes realized from using the Real Estate Foreclosure Accommodation (REFA) program, which is also called the mitigation program.

A qualified financial analyst works with this program to prepare position analysis. The financial analyst, a state certified mortgage/finance officer, should also be certified by mortgage lenders. The REFA program demands that a lender should refer to clients who are facing foreclosure possibilities or already foreclosed. The financial analyst makes relevant data, analysis checks, qualification of the tenants, and necessary recommendations for a reshuffled mortgage financing. If a tenant is already foreclosing, he or she will consult with the finance officer as soon as possible. The foreclosure tenant or a customer will actually be evaluated for the Reshuffled Mortgage Financing (RMF) program. The RMF yields lower monthly mortgage payments, partly as a result of significant reduction of interest rates. Also, the RMF requires that tenants must shed-off their other house liabilities.

The REFA Program Data, with Analysis and Regression, including to but not necessarily limited to:

1. Aggregate liabilities
2. Willingness to execute limited liability agreement, by the tenant/customer
3. Viable income
4. Durability of the income
5. Capability (sobriety, health) to maintain a job
6. Resolution of pending legal issues, if any
7. Customers character/honesty condition
8. Mortgage foreclosure insurance that protects to only the borrower.

Useful attempts need for the purposes of securing, retaining, developing and maintaining above items. The results derived from the REFA Program need to be sent to concerned lenders for a proper decision-making. The law should fix all parties to properly consider the financial records, operational analysis and concluding recommendations. For the same fee, a re-evaluation and analysis of all documents will be conducted after every six months. This will make sure that the essential activities are going in the right direction. Thus, shortly after six months, all concerned parties will receive the validated information, supporting data and expert financial recommendation.

Service Fee

Although the tenant/customer is the debtor, only the lender is required to give a token service fee of about $200 for each operation. Although, the fee is meager, it is hopped that due to the rampant nature of foreclosure, the financial analyst will work with a sizeable number of referred clients. Later (perhaps by a year) the $200 may be increased. The final result will lead to acquiring significant of money. Fee must be lower for affordability purposes. Finally, both lenders and borrowers will benefit from this program.

Advantages of the Lenders

1. Lenders retain the borrower.
2. Foreclosure loss of funds is avoided.
3. Vandalism which is rampant with unoccupied houses is avoided.
4. Over-inflated repair costs of foreclosure houses are eliminated.
5. Usual losses of property values to foreclosures are avoided.
6. Lenders receive valid data and sound recommendations now and in six months.

Advantages for the Borrowers

1. Foreclosure properties are avoided and foreclosure stresses eliminated.
2. Customers retain their homes and enjoy family peace of mind.
3. Mortgage payments become lighter and more affordable.
4. Customers receive free REFA Program and financial consulting.
5. Will receive free financial and loan management guidance.
6. Business customers will receive free revalidations after six months.

REFA Foreclosure

REFA Program should be taken seriously because they will always take care of foreclosures. Even when the country starts booming, there will still be foreclosures. In fact, the problems of foreclosures are various and the numbers of the affected individuals increase daily. For example, according to the media (ABC TV news), there are over 18 million older homeless persons and over 13.2 million homeless children in this country. However, there are over 8 million homeless persons in Los Angeles County alone.

CHAPTER TEN
Reverse Mortgage

Reverse Mortgage - Definition

Reverse mortgage is a program that offers a qualified senior mortgagor (62 years of age and above) an option to receive mortgage payments from his bank instead of making payments to his bank. The benefits with a reverse mortgage plan are more powerful when the existing economy is very difficult in the country. The program limits foreclosure with repossession for older adults. The aim of this book is not to write about reverse mortgage programs, rather, it is to show senior mortgagees of no more of mortgage payments and the limitation of foreclosure causes and repossession pains to them. Indeed, a reverse mortgage yields money for the senior mortgagees, thereby solving the needs of funds for them. Essentially, if mortgagees and their spouses are deceased, the banks sell the homes and recover the mortgage amounts paid to the home owners. This program, although generally called "reverse mortgage," is also called the "reverse home mortgage" or "reverse home equity mortgage". The Housing Urban Development (HUD) has since structured Home Equity Conversion Mortgage (HECM), a similar program to reverse mortgage. The different names of the program reflect diverse entities that associate with reverse mortgage programs.

Importance of Reverse Mortgage Are:

1. Facilitates payments from the mortgage bank to the home owner until he or she dies

2. Acquires a lump sum of money for the home owner when need arises

3. Create line of credit for the home owner to draw money from periodically

4. Extend payments to the home owner for a defined number of months or years

5. Provide reassurance of essential benefits and better living conditions to homeowners

Explanations of above statements
(Importance of Reverse Mortgage)

1. The number one statement above means that the mortgagor will receive money from the bank or financial institutions for monthly mortgage payments as long as he lives. Moreover, the same stipulation pertains to a spouse, if a mortgagor is legally married.

2. The second statement above is an option for the home owner to accept a lump sum of cash instead of receiving monthly payments. The lump sum of cash is to be paid back after the death of the home owner(s) with proceeds realized from the sale of the property.

3. Number three is frequently chosen by home owners who do not have urgent needs for cash; hence, they choose the option of opening a line of credit where they can draw money when a need arises.

4. The fourth statement is when home owners believe that they need money to set aside for months or years. Therefore, The mortgagors will opt to receive monthly payments for a specific number of months or years.

5. Number five explains that a reverse mortgage plan is better when the economy of the country is vulnerable, as in a case of a depressed or recessed economy. Undoubtedly, the program is able to afford the money which is set aside for the senior home owners to have better living conditions. A senior mortgagor, who qualifies for this program and accepts it, will be making better choices.

Each home owner with a reserve mortgage understands that the home owner must physically reside in the same home. If the home owner is deceased, the surviving spouse will continue to live in the home and receive payments until death. Property owners need to know and understand that reverse mortgage is only for private homes. The private homes are defined as single to four family homes, including qualified mobile homes.

Required Qualifications of a Senior Home Mortgagor

Mortgage requirements for Senior Home owners include:

1. Both borrower and spouse (co-owner) must be at least sixty-two years of age.
2. The home must be FHA approved. Further, it can be a unit in a four-family home which is occupied by the home owner. Also, properties such as planned unit developments, condominiums and townhouses are eligible to benefit from this program.
3. Mobile homes and other cooperatives may qualify on the condition that the owners own the land beneath the buildings.
4. The borrower and spouse (if any) must own and occupy the home as their principal residence for the rest of their lives.

5. The home must be free of debt or nearly paid-off. The balance of the home mortgage loan could be paid-off or financed in the reverse mortgage deal, through a cash draw at the home closing.

6. A home owner cannot be in bankruptcy or filing for a bankruptcy.

7. The borrowers need to attend reverse mortgage counseling through the Housing Urban Development (HUD). At completion of counseling, each participating borrower receives a certificate which will be valid for 180 days.

Advantages and Disadvantages of Reverse Mortgage

Advantages of Reserve Mortgage Include:

1. Less stress because no monthly payment is required.

2. The home owner retains title to the property.

3. Payment for the reverse mortgage will not be due when the borrower or the spouse is alive and resides in the same home as the primary residence.

4. The total payments of a home owner may not exceed the home value agreed upon.

5. If the lender/bank stops payments, the FHA will resume and continue the payments as the reverse mortgage agreement specifies, until the death of the mortgagee and/ or spouse.

6. The income of the home owner is not considered in the qualification for the program because he or she will receive money instead of making payments.

7. The mortgage lender/bank pays the real estate taxes and insurance if the home owner includes such request in the contract.

8. If the home owner has a sizeable balance of mortgage loan, a lump sum option of the reverse mortgage could be cashed out to pay-off the balance, live rent free, have fewer worries and be able to manage other stress related conditions.

Number four emphasizes that the home value in a reverse mortgage agreement is constant, as the contract stipulates. Also, if the future home value or sales becomes to a higher amount, the bank is certain to pay the amount agreed upon, by the contract. On the other hand, if for some reason the home dilapidates, the home owner does not owe the bank anything.

Number five emphasizes on a mortgagor who has lost a source of income. If a bank enters into a reverse mortgage contract and stops payments due to the fact that a mortgagor entered into bankruptcy or other unforeseen circumstances, the Federal Housing Authority (FHA) will resume and continue to pay the home owner as agreed upon, in the contract.

Number six notes that although the home owner is the applicant, it is not necessary to pull his/her credit reports because, if other qualifications go through, the home owner will receive money instead of paying money.

Number seven is a reminder to potential reverse mortgage applicant to consider including the home insurance and taxes with mortgage, for the lender to pay, before signing the agreements. This will give the home owner more financial freedom and less stress because the home insurances and taxes fluctuate sometimes.

Disadvantages of Reserve Mortgage Include:

1. Home owners pay the origination fee of 2% or $2,000, whichever is greater.
2. Home owners pay a servicing fee of not more than $35.
3. Home owners are responsible to the home maintenance if not included, for the lender in the contract.
4. Home owners are responsible for the taxes and insurances, if not included in the contract, as the responsibility of the lender.
5. Home owners pay a total closing cost of about $7,500 which includes the following:
   (a) Survey fees.
   (b) Title fees.
   (c) Origination fees.
   (d) Servicing fees.
   (e) Insurance premium.
   (f) Credit report fees.
   (g) Processing fees.
   (h) Appraisal fees.
   (i) Inspection fees.

CHAPTER ELEVEN
Definition Of Terminologies

Text Terminologies

Multiple terms and abbreviations are used in this book and add flavor to the meanings of the real estate language. Therefore, it is necessary for this chapter to define the terminologies, abbreviations and show their relative meanings as used in this text. The definition of terms in this chapter will understand the languages.

Real Estate

Real estate is often defined in multiple ways by different people or entities. Some say that real estate is a historical name for earth or land, while others believe that real estate is the earth or land beneath and above it. Also, the term "real estate" refers to physical land, accessories and structures affixed to it ("Special technical committee," 1989). Although, the definitions of real estate are not exactly the same, the terms of real estate and real property are often used synonymously in many states. Real estate is historically a term that has come about as the result of commercial practice.

Real Property

A real property is without any type of loan or mortgage attached to it.

Land

Land includes the surface of the earth, the area beneath the surface and anything permanently affixed to it.

Real Estate Buyers

Every market must have demand and supply and/or buyers and sellers. Real estate buyers are people who engage in the real estate market to find real properties. Since real property is fixed and stagnant, the market is essentially localized. Therefore, real estate buyers approach real estate sellers for assistance concerning the properties they select to buy.

Floor Price of a Home

This is the lowest price a property buyer offers to a property seller concerning a real estate property in the market.

Ceiling Price of a Home

The highest price a property buyer is willing to accept and pay for the property.

Transaction Price of a Home

This is the price acceptable by both the buyer and the seller in the real estate market. At this price, the sale or deal is transacted. In some states, the transaction price is called the contract sales price. It is very necessary that the attitude of the buyer or representative of the buyer remain diplomatic while negotiating the transaction price of a property.

Return on Investment (ROI)

This is the turnover a person expects to realize from an investment. The ratio of net profit to total assets measures the return on total investment or the ROI.

The formula to calculate the ROI is = $\dfrac{\text{Net Profit after Taxes}}{\text{Total Assets}}$

Formula: Net Profit After Taxes died by Total Assets = ROI

Net Profit

This is the Total Revenue realized when all expenses are subtracted. Other wise, it is the Gross Profit or Earnings before Taxes.

Buying Attitudes

These are the manners, conducts and behaviors a person engaging in a real estate transaction exhibits. These behaviors are often guided by emotional, mental, spiritual and physical state of the person.

Classified "A" and "B" Common Stocks

Common stocks, advantages and disadvantages, are defined in chapter seven of this book. Classified "A" common stocks are non-voting stocks. Dividend paying stocks are issued to the public. Classified "B" common stocks are non dividend paying stocks. However, they are paying stocks with voting rights issued to the management of the enterprise. These stocks give them control of the corporation affairs.

Convertible Preferred Stocks

These are the preferred stocks that a home owner can purchase and reserve the right to convert them into common stocks at a specified date in the future.

Convertible Bond

A home owner could purchase some bonds and reserve the right to convert them into other shares at a specified date in the future.

Secured Bonds

These are different types of bonds, such as serial and long-term. A home owner may like to purchase secured bonds with his or her cashed-out funds from a home equity. Secured bonds are secured with the asset of the issuing company because they are sheltered.

Mortgage Bonds

These bonds are secured with real estates hoping that the home owners will invest in the bonds.

Debentures

Debentures are bonds that are secured with the prestige of the issuing company. Nevertheless, both small and big companies can go broke, with this type of investment.

Municipal Bonds

Municipal bonds are issued by a municipal or a local government. The owners of municipal bonds do not pay taxes on the proceeds. Municipal bonds are good sources of investments.

Deed

A deed is a written contract through which legal title to a property is conveyed from the seller to the buyer. A deed is a very powerful instrument that is encountered during the sale of real estate property. A deed usually contains names, addresses and signatures of both parties (sellers and purchasers). A deed must describe the property being communicated. Of course, both parties must be adults (or emancipated) and contractually capable of executing business transactions. In other words, all participants must be of legal age, health and willing.

Deed of Trust

A deed of trust is an instrument used in lieu of a mortgage, to convey the title of real property to a third party in trust; while the debtor repays the debt to the lender. The primary advantage of this instrument is that it assists the lender to foreclose faster and easier than an ordinary mortgage deed. The borrower may transfer title to a trustee. However, in the event of a default, the trustee may foreclose on the mortgage and sell the property without going through the usual court foreclosure process. The deed of trust serves the same purpose as a regular mortgage. A mortgage is a pledge of a specific asset as security for a debt. People need to remember that a deed of trust expedites transactions more than the foreclosure activities processed by the court systems. A borrower who operates under a deed of trust is known as the trust-or, while the mortgage lender becomes the beneficiary. Consequently, the third party is the trustee. It is not very advantageous for a home buyer to accept a deed of trust.

Trustee

A trustee in the mortgage business is the person assigned to the property, to ensure that the borrower performs his or her obligations effectively.

Option

This is the right given to a buyer to chase a form. The buyer may chase to purchase or lease a property in accordance to the terms specified in the contract.

Balloon Mortgage Contract

Balloon Contract and land mortgage contract are discussed in details in chapter six.

Default

Mortgage default occurs when a home owner fails to make any type of property payment agreed upon in the real estate contract.

Appreciation

Appreciation is the increase in monetary value of a property, over time. Real estate property is an asset that can appreciate. After owning a house for some years, the value of the house increases contingent on proper maintenance of the property. Thus, the home owner retains more financial equity in the property which, may be cashed-out and reinvested in the same property or used in other ways.

Depreciation

Depreciation is the opposite of appreciation. Generally, assets decrease in worth and/ or monetary value over time. In finance or accounting and asset that depreciate, yield money which is set aside from income before realizing a taxable profit. The purpose of setting money aside is to assist in replacing the asset when it becomes old and/or depleted. The Internal Revenue Service (IRS) allows depreciation for the economic life of the asset.

Lien or Pledge

A lien or pledge on a property, gives a creditor the right to petition the court about selling the assets of a debtor in other to satisfy default payments of that debtor. The court may approve foreclosure or assign a receivership to the debtor.

Receivership

A receivership means that the court appoints someone (receiver) to collect and disburse funds monthly or as the court prescribes to creditors.

Real Estate Closing

This is the final transaction meeting between buyer, seller and title agency. At this time, the deed and money are exchanged for the sale of the property. Legally, the title company is the only agency in charge of a real estate closing transaction.

Delayed Closing

This is the closing of a real estate purchase loan after it has been delayed. Under this condition, a buyer agrees to buy the property and complete the closing of the same property, at a future date.

Closing Statement

A closing statement is a written report itemizing the responsibilities of the buyer, seller and mortgage lender in respect to taxes, insurances, interest rates, commissions and other significant expenses. Both buyer and seller must sign this document and receive copies for their personal files.

Void Contract

This is a contract that is nullified because it does not satisfy all the necessary legal aspects.

Voidable Contract

A voidable contract includes:

- An acquisition without a consideration is voidable.
- A person who is mentally challenged enters into a contract.
- A contract with a minor or juvenile is voidable except if the juvenile is emancipated.

Consideration

This is the value given up by the buyer to acquire something of importance.

Exchange Theory

In real estate activities, one may exchange one property with another property. The main reason for this is to obtain maximum tax shelter. However, the properties to exchange must be of equal value.

Home Equity

Home equity is the monetary value of a home at a specific time and date.

Home Equity Line of Credit (HELOC)

This is a second mortgage that a borrower assumes; which establishes the value of the property. A home owner with HELOC is allowed to periodically withdraw money from the line of credit up to the limit of the amount that the contract establishes. This money may go to resolve anything the home owner desires; usually loan interest is charged only on the amount of money withdrawn. This is another way a home owner receives and invests the proceeds from a home equity. This type of line of credit is popularly known as HELOC.

Warranty Deed

A warranty deed is a written guarantee of the condition of a property. Generally, warranties have limitation or expiration dates.

Assets

Assets are the belongings of a person with present and future values.

Liability

This is the opposite of assets. Liability is something a person owes or obligations (debts) a person owes to a third party.

Legacy

Legacy is a bequest or inheritance of money or other personal property a person receives mostly via a will.

Price of a Property

This is the agreed upon value of a property under a specified system of exchange, such as money or another property.

Prima Facie

This means that everything is regarded as correct until proven false.

Ceteris Paribus

Ceteris paribus is referred to as all things being equal. This means that activities will be completed as planned if there are no emergencies or unforeseen circumstances.

Dower Rights

These are interests a person earns from the property or estate of a spouse.

CHAPTER TWELVE
SUMMARY

This book begins with the introduction of the title page, copyright, dedication, acknowledgement and table of contents. The text describes real estate industry, main objectives, author-remarks, text tables, figures and other participants. They are well discussed. Also, this book elaborates how potential information obtains from engaging with mortgage activities. Actually, the book enhances a person's knowledge, skills and abilities in the areas of practices, purchases, selling and other broader techniques. Studies show that mortgage loans used for the purchase of homes/houses are the biggest financial commitments made by mostly families. Therefore, the need to have a home becomes prevalence in all societies or cultures.

There are two most important plans in this book. The first is the plans and actions "Before", "During" and "After" Mortgage Financing. The "Before" is the Mortgage Financing, the "During" is Sources of Financing Classification and "After" is monthly Mortgage Payments and maintenance of the real estate property. The second is the Effects on Mortgage Foreclosure with Repossession which shows Remote and Immediate Causes. Further, the mortgage risks, credit issues, judgments and types of frauds are explained and illustrated with examples. The sources and levels of funds are also explained. Examples of mortgage products, land contracts and balloon contracts are clarified.

Different types of homes, apartment complexes, town houses, duplex buildings and condominiums are detailed. The existing programs that enhance the real estate industry and suggestions on how to improve their efficacies are presented. Examples of these programs are the Real Estate Foreclosure Accommodation (REFA) program, Reshuffled Mortgage Financing (RMF), Reverse Mortgage Program (RMP), Reverse Mortgage, Customer Mortgage Insurance Program (CMIP), Title Insurance for Lender (TIL), Title Insurance for Borrowers (TIB), Home Mortgage Disclosure Act (HDMA), diagrams, figures and tables are used to fully decorate and enhance proper understanding of this book. Next, terminologies used in this text are defined to assist and understand real estate language as used in the text. The tables of book parts are listed.

Table Of Book Parts

The contents of this book are separated into five parts. The book contains a total of twelve chapters. Also, it shows that the book parts will be easy for readers to see what they may be interested.

PART ONE

Part one contains the initial cover of the chapters. Part one contains the following:

Title page

Dedication page

Copyright page

Acknowledgement page

Table of Contents

Overview of the Chapters

Summary of Tables and Figures

PART TWO

Part two covers chapters one, two and three. This section also introduces the chapters in the book and gives the analysis of contents in each chapter. Finally, it contains valuable information about preliminary and real estate transactions.

PART THREE

Part three of this book composes on chapters four, five, six and seven. It contains effective and rewarding techniques concerning real estate dealings. Further, it outlines plans and actions to use before, during and after a real estate mortgage financing. Lastly, it highlights the type of frauds that exist in the real estate industry.

PART FOUR

Part four contains chapters eight, nine and ten. This section deals with the causes, consequences and remedies or controls of foreclosure with repossession pains. Also, it introduces the idea of Re-shuffled Mortgage Financing (RMF) and comments on the Revised Mortgage.

PART FIVE

Part five includes chapter eleven and twelve. It identifies the terminologies used in this book. Chapter eleven is necessary to show the interpretations of terms as they pertain on the contents of the book. Finally, the last chapter shows the text references and the book parts.

Bibliography

ABC News. (2009). 6:30 p.m. News cast, Dayton, Ohio.

Alderfer, C. P. (1972). Existence, Relatedness, Growth: Human Needs in Organizational Settings, New York, New York: Free Press.

Amling, F. (1981). Investments, 2nd ed., Englewood Cliffs, New Jersey: Prentice-Hall, Inc.,

Beaton, W. R. (1982). Real Estate Finance, Englewood Cliffs, New Jersey, Prentice-Hall, Inc.

Certo, S. C. (2003). Modern Management, 9th ed., Upper Saddle River, New Jersey, Pearson Education, Inc.

Committee on Financial Services, Consumer Mortgage Coalition, Subcommittee on Housing and Community Opportunity, U S House of Representatives. (1984).

Czerwinski (2000). HUD'S Government-Insured Mortgages: The Problem Of Property Flipping, Permanent Subcommittee On Investigations, United States Senate.

Donahue, Sr. K. M. (2000). HUD Inspector General, HUD'S Government-Insured Mortgages: The Problem of Property "Flipping," Permanent Subcommittee On Investigations, United States Senate, One hundred sixth Congress, 2nd. Session.

Dayton Area Board of Realtor, 1515 South Main Street, Dayton, Ohio 45409,(2010).

Goulet, P. G. (1979). Real Estate: A Value Approach, Encino, California: Glencoe Publishing Company, Inc.

Guttentag, J. & Igor, R. (2009). MPI and the future of the housing finance system, Prudent Lending Restored, (Securitization After the Mortgage Meltdown), Washington, DC: Brookings Institution Press.

Hoagland, H. E., & Leo D. S. (1972). Real Estate Finance, 4th ed., Richard D. Irwin, Inc.

Hondros. (2009). Mortgage Loan Originator, Published by Hondros Learning, United States of America.

Igah, F. M. (1983). The Effects of A Depressed Economy on the demand For Single Family Homes, Dayton, Ohio: UGS, Cincinnati, (Dissertation).

Jacobus, C. J. (1999). Real Estate Principles, 8th.ed. Upper Saddle River, New Jersey: Simon & Schuster/A Viacom Company.

Jordan, D. F. & Dowgall, H. E. (1960). I n v e s t m e n t s, 7th ed., New York, New York: Englewood Cliffs, New Jersey, Prentice-Hall, Inc.

Kearns, M. P. (1994). The Law Of Real Property, Albany, New York: Delmar Publishers, Inc.

Knowles, J. Jr. (1967). Single Family Residential Appraisal Manual, Chicago, Illinois: Lakeside Press, R. R. Donnelley & Sons Company.

LaFay, B. & Barrell, D. (2003). Reverse Mortgage For Senior Homeowners, Chicago, Illinois: Dearborn Real Estate Education.

Malone, L. A. (1986). How to Avoid Foreclosure, White Hall, Virginia: Better way Publications, Inc.

Maslow, A. H. (1954). Motivation and Personality, New York, New York: Harper E. Brothers.

McCall, M. (2004). Fraud In Our Nation's Mortgage Industry, Committee On Financial Services, United House Of Representatives.

McClelland, D. C. (1992). Scoring Manual For the Achievement Motives, New York, New York: Cambridge University Press.

McGowan, K. & Hester, J. A. Jr. (1962). Early Man In The New World, Garden City, New York: Doubleday and Company, Inc.

Miller, G. H. & Gilbeau, K. W. (1980). An Introduction To Real Estate Appraising, Englewood Cliffs, New Jersey, Prentice-Hall, Inc.

Pearson, K. G. & Litka, M.P. (2013) Real Estate: Principles and Practices, 3rd. Ed. Grid Columbus, OH Grid Publishing Inc.

Prieston, A.J. (2004). Mortgage Fraud and It's Impact on Mortgage Lenders; Subcommittee on Financial Housing and Community, United States House of Representatives.

Public Broadcasting System (Jim. B.). 2013. Market Place: radio station

Ring, A. A., Dasso, J. (1977). Real Estate Principles and Practices 8th Ed. Englewood Cliffs NJ, Prentice-Hall, Inc.

Scott. (2000). Government-Insured Mortgages; The Problem of Property Flipping Permanent Subcommittee on Investigations. United States Senate.

Special Technical Committee. (1970). The Appraisal of Real Estate. Chicago, IL American Lakeside Press.

Train Pro, (2009). Applying Mortgage Knowledge to Exam Preparation. United States of America: Advanced Education System, LLC.

Weicher, (2010). HUD's Government-Insured Mortgages; The Problem of Property Flipping Permanent Subcommittee on Investigations. United States Senate.

Unger, M.A., Karvel, G.R. (1979). Real Estate Principles and Practices. Cincinnati, OH: South Western Pub Company.

White, D. (2008). White Appraisal Services. Greenville OH.

Printed in the United States
By Bookmasters